©2025 Relatomics Foundation & Angello
All rights reserved.

ISBN 978-969-9492-71-6

angello

AN APOSTOLIC NETWORK OF AGENTS FOR CHANGE

Foreword

In a world that often separates faith from enterprise and profit from purpose, Angello: An Apostolic Network of Agents for Change presents a radically different vision, one in which ordinary people have discovered that their work is their ministry, their business is a sacred act of service, and entrepreneurship is a divine calling to contribute towards a global platform for transformational change.

This book is a collection of case studies of the experiences of members of a movement towards the realisation of biblical principles for community through commerce. We invite you to discover some of the hearts and minds that fuel the Angello network, a vibrant alliance of faith-driven entrepreneurs, apostolic leaders and changemakers working in nations with emerging markets.

We believe that enterprise is not merely an economic strategy; it is a God-given system that allows anyone, anywhere, to fulfil their purpose, discover meaning and identity in relationships, and build unity across all people and places. Through enterprise we believe that the kingdom of heaven, a place of love, peace, joy and relational harmony, is being realised and can be scaled to heal the needs of nations, today.

What you'll find in these pages is more than theory, self-help tips or personal inspiration. These are living stories of ordinary men and women who intentionally bring their Christ-led perspective, principles and practice into the marketplace every day, leading ventures with courage and humility, and pursuing justice and impact through their businesses despite challenges, failures and the deceit of worldly success. They do not walk alone. They walk together in community - an Acts Community - rooted in the values of Fellowship, Discipleship, Joy, Generosity, Service and Impact.

As you spend time with these stories, our hope is that you will feel and hear the call of a new heaven and new earth emerging in today's world. Each story bears witness to the evidence of servant leadership in action, sometimes costly, always faithful. We hope you will be challenged to reimagine what is possible when your work and business become vessels for pouring out love, hope and mercy to those around you and across the world.

May these stories stir your spirit and draw you into a deeper understanding of what it means to live for and lead something greater than yourself through your existing resources, context, skills and relationships. May these acts of modern-day apostolic leaders, called to spread the teachings of Jesus Christ through a principled marketplace, encourage you to write your own chapter of the ongoing story of the Book of Acts.

Join us for the journey.

Dr Colin Habberton
Angello Partner
Cape Town, South Africa
October 2025

Contents

Chapter One: Introduction
Our Purpose and Beliefs..2
Our Vision: A Future Fueled by Enterprise..3

Chapter Two: The Expressions of Angello Over Time
Acts Community...5
Being and Doing..8
The Angello Development Foundation..10
Our Tribe..12
Investor Network...13
The Global Youth Network..14
FORGE..15
Angello Netwrok..16
Angello Innovation Lab...17

Chapter Three: Agents for Change
Fellowship with Malcolm Johnston and Artem Magay................19
Discipleship with Paul Lindsay and Roy Crowne.........................36
Hospitality with Ralph Catto, Luvuyo Rani & Colin Habberton..54
Discernment with Reuben Coulter..74
Service with Duncan Parker and Kehkshan Newton...................90
Obedience with Hakan Sandberg and Manpan Wungak........105
Justice with Nikolaus Hutter and Edson Niwamanya...............123
Integrity with Derek Kessen and Anatol Malancea...................142
Transformation with Ruben Marian and Daniel Lar.................159
Impact with Smily Rostus...176
Generosity with David Harlley and Keren Pybus........................190
Joy with Mason Tan..206

Appendix One: Contributors
Malcolm Johnston & Artem Magay......................................225
Paul Lindsay & Roy Crowne..226
Ralph Catto, Luvuyo Rani & Colin Habberton.....................228
Reuben Coulter..230
Duncan Parker & Kehkshan Newton....................................231
Hakan Sandberg & Manpan Wungak...................................233
Nikolaus Hutter & Edson Niwamanya.................................234
Derek Kessen & Anatol Malancea..236
Ruben Marian & Daniel Lar..239
Smily Rostus..241
David Harlley & Keren Pybus...243
Mason Tan...245

Chapter One: Introduction

Angello was launched in 2010, with the aim of fostering a nurturing, ethical environment in which faith-driven leaders can thrive both spiritually and economically, all the while contributing to meaningful, transformative change across the globe. The Angello network was inspired by the early church model of the Apostles in the Book of the Acts, and fosters a vibrant community built on generosity, collaboration, spiritual growth and shared purpose. It is a fellowship of visionary leaders operating at local and national levels across nations with emerging 'frontier' markets seeking and needing investment.

Angello is more than a network. It is a vibrant alliance of changemakers, entrepreneurs and faith-driven leaders committed to empowering developing nations through enterprise and income generation. Through catalytic investment, capacity building and a deep-rooted commitment to social transformation, Angello fosters sustainable ventures in 'frontier' nations with a mission-driven approach, enabling families and communities to thrive financially, socially and spiritually.

At the heart of Angello is a coalition of emerging market leaders with vast expertise in investment and commercial, government and civil society initiatives. All have a shared conviction that business and faith together can change the world. Angello partners with international apostolic leaders to enable entrepreneurial ecosystems to grow in emerging markets. The goal is not just to teach people to fish, but to empower them to feed their communities for a lifetime.

In this book, Angello's commitment is captured in twelve

deeply personal case studies drawn from conversations with men and women who bring their faith into the heart of their business practice. Their stories reveal how faith shapes decisions, redefines success, and transforms relationships with staff, investors, customers and communities. They offer an inspirational roadmap for stewarding influence in ways that honour God and serve others. At the forefront of this movement is the intention to operate as an Acts Community — a modern-day expression of the early church. These entrepreneurs are brothers and sisters in Christ who believe they are called to carry Kingdom values into every sphere of their influence. This modern-day Acts Community is not driven by hierarchy or performance, but by unity, generosity and purpose.

"The book of Acts isn't done, because 2025 years later we're still writing it. That whole idea that we're an Acts Community ... I think that's what Angello's about - recognizing when other people are doing them and going, 'We're still doing that.'" - Duncan Parker

Angello embodies a mission-driven approach inspired by the model of the early Church in the Book of Acts, centred on generosity, trust, and shared purpose. We exist to nurture faith-aligned enterprises that generate sustainable jobs, restore dignity, and catalyse long-term community impact.

Our Purpose and Beliefs

At Angello, we believe enterprise is a God-given tool for transformation. Our purpose is rooted in the conviction that lasting impact comes not from handouts, but from hope, opportunity and enterprise-led development. We believe enterprise-led development is a necessity in nations with emerging "frontier" markets seeking investment, and where aid has not delivered long-term economic renewal. We champion business as a force for good, empowering individuals, families and communities to flourish. We invest not just money, but time, wisdom, prayer and presence, mobilising capital and relationships to grow businesses that honour God and serve people.

Our inspiration is drawn from the early believers in the Book of the Acts of the Apostles, a community marked by faith, generosity, joy and service which had 'impact' - that is, a measurably positive effect upon the activities and lives of others.

The Acts Community is our spiritual and relational backbone. It values honest relationships over polite proximity, collaboration over competition, and giving over gaining. It holds space for transformation, where strong leaders choose vulnerability and where faith meets enterprise to bring about real change. We believe true flourishing integrates Purpose, People, Planet, and Profit. When business is done God's way, communities transform and hope rises. In all we do, we are led by a core set of Acts values, namely Fellowship, Discipleship, Joy, Generosity, Service and Impact.

Our Vision: A Future Fuelled by Enterprise and the Acts Community

We envision vibrant communities empowered by self-sustaining enterprises that promote collaboration and shared prosperity. Through our work, we build networks that foster growth, accountability, and social responsibility, creating environments where everyone can contribute meaningfully. This future is already unfolding — one enterprise, one community, one act of obedience at a time.

At the heart of this unfolding vision lies the Acts Community, the spiritual heartbeat of Angello — a fellowship of believers carrying the DNA of the early church into the marketplace. The first Apostles responded to Jesus' commission with boldness and unity; similarly, the Angello network of Acts Community entrepreneurs respond to God's call to meet needs and transform lives, doing so through enterprise.

The early church was built by people of diverse backgrounds united by purpose. They didn't theorise, they acted. Similarly, Angello entrepreneurs test, adapt and learn as they go, shaping real-world responses to pressing challenges. Angello was born from the realisation that to walk this path well, we need one another. Entrepreneurs are often fiercely independent, but true growth comes through vulnerability, accountability and shared purpose.

"To dare and to endure — this is the spirit of our fellowship."

Acts Communities offer a countercultural space where driven leaders choose humility, accountability and mutual support. They reflect the essence of the early church which remains essential today.

We are not building faith through ritual or structure, but by returning to the simplicity and power of 1st century discipleship, lived through everyday decisions in business and community.

Acts Communities are living experiments in Kingdom life. We learn by doing, testing bold ideas, adjusting with wisdom and following the Spirit's lead. Above all, the Communities are spaces of belonging and transformation where lonely leaders find kinship, and shared faith becomes shared purpose. Together, we are still writing the book of Acts, and we invite you to join us.

Chapter Two:
The Expressions
of Angello Over Time

The Acts Community

Acts Communities in many ways resemble the powerhouse of energy and ministry that was the early Apostles: Diversified personalities, skills and experiences, but unified in their calling to follow Him. When Jesus had left them, commissioning them with a clear but daunting task, they went on extending and translating what they had seen Him do into breaking new ground, meeting needs, solving problems, and growing the impact by His authority, on their mission throughout the world. Entrepreneurs in many ways carry that apostolic role or function in today's society, stretching forward, meeting needs, and solving problems, and the Acts Communities are fellowships of brothers and sisters supporting one another in spearheading His kingdom life into the marketplace, for the transformation of people and societies.

The first Apostles were followed by many apostolic leaders over many years and generations, who through their lives implemented the kingdom life in all relationships and spheres of influence, and a movement was born that we are still a part of today. As most entrepreneurial leaders, they are by design equipped with a strong will and determination, which makes it challenging for them to choose dependency and vulnerability in relation to others. But that is exactly what we need to walk in step with Jesus, and survive the lonely and targeted position as entrepreneurs.

We believe that God-fearing, Jesus-following entrepreneurs will carry much of the kingdom influence into both our own nations and contexts, but also into the not yet reached part of the world. That is still the same daunting task, and Jesus is still the one who "has been given all authority in heaven and on earth", and commissioned us to go and extend His work. That is why this mission is still relevant today and why we should still pursue it.

To build unity in the matrix of diversity, we need to scale back all the extra curricula we have built around faith and following and come back to the very beginning, to imagine the focus and life of the first Apostles. To build a "1st century apostolic/entrepreneurial community in the 21st century marketplace", and we call that Acts Communities.

What could this look like in reality? Six values distilled from the text in Acts 2:42-47 are the foundation we build the Acts Community groups on. The text reads: *"They devoted themselves to the apostles' teaching and to fellowship, to the breaking of bread and to prayer. Everyone was filled with awe at the many wonders and signs performed by the apostles. All the believers were together and had everything in common. They sold property and possessions to give to anyone who had need. Every day they continued to meet together in the temple courts. They broke bread in their homes and ate together with glad and sincere hearts, praising God and enjoying the favour of all the people. And the Lord added to their number daily those who were being saved."*

We named the values; Fellowship, Discipleship, Joy, Generosity, Service and Impact.

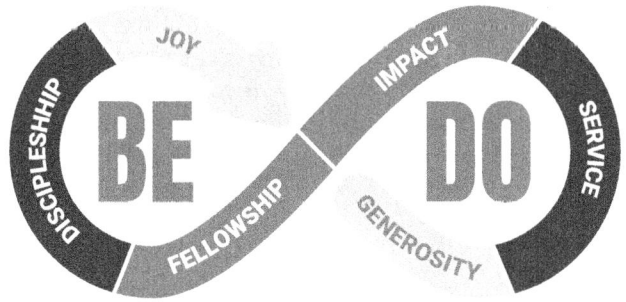

Those values are each based on a principle:

- Fellowship - the principle of sharing life
- Discipleship - the principle of journeying together
- Joy - the principle of giving thanks
- Generosity - the principle of living abundantly
- Service - the principle of loving sacrificially
- Impact - the principle of leading courageously

That all sounds good but a bit theoretical, doesn't it? How do we bring this into our everyday lives? What could this look like in a local group of entrepreneurs sharing fellowship with one another? Suggested practices are:

- Sharing life through eating and praying together.
- Journeying together through walking deeply with Christ, then challenging one another, leading to transformation
- Giving thanks through celebrating the good by sharing stories
- Living abundantly through sharing resources freely and investing thoughtfully
- Loving sacrificially through always empowering others, sometimes through mentoring or coaching
- Leading courageously through pioneering new things, but also through cultivating what has been started

These are not prescriptive practices but suggestions to start with whilst you create your contextual expression of an Acts Community. In each group and in each culture or context, the values can be expressed through a variety of practices that look, feel and taste differently but translate the values into action. We believe that business, at the core of it, is love expressed in action, because love is a verb. The Acts Communities are a safe place where entrepreneurs can grow deeper in God's love and shape the expressions of it through their lives and businesses.

Being and Doing

The apostolic function of the entrepreneur often tends to make us single minded **doers**. That over time can tend to wear us down and is not a sustainable lifestyle. We need to balance the doing with **being**. That is the constant rhythm of drawing near to God, being present with him to listen, and to fellowship, hearing his heart and being transformed into his likeness, and from that place of rest, to go out expressing his love and presence in action, the **doing**. That rhythm is how God created everything. There is always this balance between resting and activity. Look at the lungs, the breathing, the heart pulse, day and night, and the seasons of winter and spring, both resting and blooming.

We need those amongst us that keep reminding us about these rhythms, and especially the "being" part that is the most difficult for us. This is a typical prophetic function and it prevents us from "mission drift", forgetting our "why", and helps us calibrate our hearts with God's heart so we are truly led by the Spirit in our everyday lives and at work.

So then, if you get inspired to be part of an Acts Community group, where can you find it? The answer is that you start it where you are! It begins with **you**. You cannot inspire anyone else to live this Acts Community life unless you yourself live it. That is a journey, and probably a lifelong one, but we can at least start and get used to some of the values, perhaps starting with the ones that speak the most to us. Which of the practices can you integrate in your life when you are alone, before you have a group to practice with? Be creative and do this with a few of them.

And then, pray that God will let you find one more entrepreneur who is longing for such a fellowship of like-mindedness. Perhaps this may be someone who is stronger on the "being" side if you're more of a "doer", who will allow you to encourage one another and grow in the practices where they excel and you need growth. As the the two of you connect, pray for one more entrepreneur, and from there, just let it ripple. When you are three praying in unity and sharing life with one another, it becomes contagious, and others will be drawn to you if you are open for that. Be relaxed about it and let it ripple; making sure that this is born out of need and desire, rather than through pushing a program to grow. Life lived together should grow deep roots before it grows wide.

Many entrepreneurs can struggle to find their place in the Church. There doesn't seem to be a role for them there, so they express themselves in the marketplace, where they make perfect sense. However, ultimately our calling is about the kingdom of God, and we all need one another. We are created in community, by a tri-union God – to create in community, with the body of Christ – for community, the world that God loves. The apostolic gift, together with the prophetic gift, was given to the Church, and the Church was built on that foundation, as outlined in Ephesians 2:20. The Acts Communities helps entrepreneurs find their role and exercise it with boldness. Yet it is also a gift to the wider Church, alongside the other ministry gifts described in Ephesians 4:11-12. Our task is to find ways of reintegrating those often-missing gifts back into the life of the Church. With the support of one another, we can take steps in that direction, by growing in patience and generosity as we offer our service and our hearts to Kingdom work, joining with other members of the body in our local contexts.

Our particular role as entrepreneurs is to bless the city. We are uniquely positioned to understand the city, its language, its drivers, and the challenges it faces. God has entrusted us with minds and tools to create solutions, echoing His own creativity in doing so. As Jeremiah 29:7 reminds us, *"Also, seek the peace and prosperity of the city to which I have carried you into exile. Pray to the LORD for it, because if it prospers, you too will prosper."* When we bring solutions to the city's needs, we are as most like our creator God who made us in his image. That is our calling, and we do that at home first, our own Jerusalem, and then to the ends of the world.

That is acting as a community – an Acts Community.

Where could you start? And who could journey with you?

The Angello Development Foundation

The Angello Development Foundation (ADF) was established as a practical response to one of the greatest challenges in frontier markets: access to capital. These are places where traditional investment rarely dares to go, and yet where the potential for transformation is the greatest. For more than a decade, ADF has been channelling resources into pioneering entrepreneurs, demonstrating that faith-driven capital can both generate returns as well as catalyse renewal.

To date, the Foundation has invested over £500,000 through loans and equity in 18 early-stage businesses across emerging markets. These ventures include a CrossFit gym and agri-loan initiative in Central Asia, modular housing manufacturing in Moldova, low-income housing in Kenya, and a fish farm in Russia. Each supported initiative reflects ADF's conviction that entrepreneurship is not only about providing livelihoods, but also about embodying kingdom values in local communities.

Intentionally structured as a closed fund, ADF does not actively promote external investment, though it occasionally welcomes aligned partners into select opportunities. Its strategy is relational and long-term — walking alongside entrepreneurs as they grow. Already, several loans have been fully repaid, evidence that the model is both viable and sustainable. Of the current portfolio, 12 businesses are progressing well, one is delayed, and one has closed, underscoring both the promise and the risks inherent in frontier investing.

At its heart, ADF pursues a quadruple bottom line: financial viability, social impact, environmental responsibility, and spiritual transformation. It prioritises businesses that are scalable, replicable, and led by entrepreneurs who can become national role models in their sectors. This vision aligns with the Nairobi Declaration (2023) for Frontier Market Investing, which calls for:

1. Catalyzing shalom — the flourishing of individuals and societies.
2. Investing through intentional communities of national entrepreneurs.
3. Developing leaders in the crucible of business.
4. Prioritising scalable and replicable models that create generational impact.

The Angello Development Foundation (ADF) exists to nurture entrepreneurs in frontier markets, equipping them to become leaders who embody kingdom values and inspire change in their societies. More than a financial mechanism, ADF is a community of mentorship, discipleship, and thought leadership that walks alongside entrepreneurs as they navigate the challenges of growth. Its strategy is relational and long-term, emphasising leadership formation, business integrity, and community renewal.

For over a decade, ADF has invested deeply in people as much as in ventures, recognising that entrepreneurship is not simply about livelihoods but about shaping culture and fostering shalom – the flourishing of individuals and societies. Entrepreneurs supported by ADF are encouraged to see themselves as national role models, carrying the potential to catalyse transformation that extends well beyond their own enterprises. This vision aligns with the Nairobi Declaration (2023) for Frontier Market Investing, which calls for developing leaders in the crucible of business, prioritising scalable and replicable models, and investing through intentional communities of local entrepreneurs.

While ADF provides catalytic capital where traditional investors hesitate, its greater contribution lies in accompanying entrepreneurs with wisdom, prayer, and relational support. It has supported initiatives as diverse as modular housing in Moldova, agri-loan schemes in Central Asia, accessible housing in Kenya, and a fish farm in Russia – each one a context for mentoring leaders who can carry both business and spiritual responsibility. Several of these ventures have already repaid loans, evidence not only of financial viability but also of the resilience and faithfulness cultivated through this journey.

At its heart, ADF pursues a quadruple bottom line: financial viability, social impact, environmental responsibility, and spiritual transformation. By fostering businesses that are outward-looking and generational in vision, the Foundation seeks to restore dignity, generate sustainable jobs, and catalyse long-term renewal. Its approach is not without risk – navigating financial controls, regulations, and the occasional failed venture – yet ADF sees these challenges as part of the process of stewardship and learning.

Ultimately, the Foundation's mission is to invest in people and ideas that matter. Capital becomes a form of discipleship, a resource stewarded not merely for financial return but for the flourishing of communities. In this way, ADF is shaping a new generation of leaders who live out their faith with courage and integrity, proving that business, when infused with purpose, can be a powerful force for transformation.

Our Tribe

The Angello Tribe is a group of 10 apostolic entrepreneurs who found each other over a period of 5 or 6 years who agreed to travel and dream together. It was born out of the realisation that we all carried that same calling and needed the support of one another to dare and to endure. Our mission has become to enable entrepreneurial ecosystems to grow in emerging markets, through national apostolic leaders.

The Angello Tribe is more than a platform or professional alliance; it is a faith-driven movement and fellowship committed to enterprise, generosity, and transformation who agreed to explore what an Acts Community could look like. At its heart, Angello exists to cultivate kingdom-centred entrepreneurship and foster business solutions for people and planet. It creates ecosystems where entrepreneurs — particularly in underserved and frontier markets — can thrive through access to mentorship, capital, encouragement and community. It inspires bold action through storytelling, intentional relationships and shared vision. Grounded in faith, Angello champions counter-cultural living, calling its members to a deeper way of engaging the world trough service, generosity, and collaborative leadership. Ultimately, Angello is a collective expression of faith in action — a global family of leaders who believe that transforming economies begins with transforming hearts and mindsets, together.

The Angello Tribe are dedicated to supporting faith-driven entrepreneurs in building businesses that reflect Godly principles and create positive change within their communities. It provides a platform for entrepreneurs to connect, share experiences and support one another on their journeys.

The Angello Tribe and their extended networks are united by values that reflect the character of Christ and the mission of the Kingdom. These shared values not only guide business operations but shape the fabric of a network where leaders walk together, support one another and boldly pursue a vision of business that reflects God's heart for justice, dignity and community.

Investor Network

The Angello Investor Network was created to bring together like-minded investors who share a passion for frontier markets and a conviction that capital can be mobilized as a force for kingdom impact. Unlike many investment forums where the agenda is shaped by the Global North, the Investor Network is a space where the voices, priorities, and experiences of the Global South set the direction.

Rooted in the principles of the Nairobi Declaration (2023) on

Frontier Market Investing, the Investor Network rejects the extractive patterns of traditional capital flows and instead champions a relational, trust-based approach to investment. It seeks to align capital with the national visions of entrepreneurs and leaders in emerging markets, ensuring that resources flow to where they are most needed — not simply where risk-adjusted returns look most attractive on paper.

Members of the Investor Network walk together in discernment, sharing opportunities, and co-investing in businesses that embody the quadruple bottom line: financial sustainability, social impact, environmental stewardship, and spiritual transformation. By intentionally focusing on scalable and replicable ventures, the Network aims to multiply the impact of every investment and fuel the growth of entrepreneurial ecosystems that can shape nations.

The Investor Network is also a learning community. Investors are encouraged to immerse themselves in frontier contexts, to understand the realities entrepreneurs face, and to allow these experiences to reshape their own perceptions of risk, value, and wealth. In doing so, the Network embodies Angello's belief that investing is not merely a financial activity but a spiritual discipline — an act of stewardship that seeks shalom for people and places often overlooked by global markets. This is a work in progress with a strong vision for what is needed. In time, the Investor Network aspires to become a catalytic movement: a global fellowship of investors who are committed to flipping the script of capital, so that frontier markets are no longer at the periphery of investment but at the centre of a new vision for redemptive enterprise.

The Global Youth Network

The Global Youth Network was developed out of a simple but urgent conviction: the future of all nations rests in the hands of their young people. Emerging markets are home to the fastest-growing youth populations in the world, yet young leaders often find themselves excluded from decision-making, underfunded, and without the support systems needed to flourish. This initiative, seeks to change that story. It is a fellowship of young entrepreneurs, innovators, and visionaries who are committed to being leaders who bring both impact and transformation. Rather than waiting for permission to lead, these young people are given the platform, mentorship, and community they need to act boldly in their own contexts. The Network connects youth leaders across nations, allowing them to share experiences, exchange knowledge, and build solidarity across borders. It provides training in entrepreneurial leadership, access to networks of investors and mentors, and opportunities to contribute their voices into the wider Angello movement. By doing so, it cultivates a new generation of leaders who not only dream but also execute — leaders who embody resilience, creativity, and faith-driven conviction. For many participants, the Network represents more than skills and resources; it is a place of belonging where young leaders discover that their struggles and hopes are shared by peers in other nations, and where they are encouraged to persist in building businesses that create jobs, dignity, and opportunity in their communities.

The Global Youth Network is still experimental and strongly visionary. Over time, it aspires to become a launching ground for national movements – equipping young people to start enterprises, but to influence culture, shape policy, and carry the values of the Acts Community into every sphere of society.

FORGE

FORGE is a movement focussed on emerging markets and led by emerging market leaders. It is a community of believers who are driving change through business in some of the world's most dynamic yet underserved contexts. More than a conference, FORGE is an immersive experience where culture, faith, entrepreneurship, and opportunity intersect. Participants explore, learn, and are inspired through worship, plenary sessions, workshops, mentorship opportunities, and cultural engagement. They connect with others God has planted around the world who share a passion and a calling for business as mission.

Following the Summit, select training and acceleration organizations are invited to FORGE Construct, a two-day intensive designed for deeper engagement. This off-site program includes practical workshops and collaborative sessions addressing the specific needs of partner organizations. The movement is intentionally emerging-market led: accessible, authentic, and owned by local leaders, and shares a vision of global partners joining in supportive roles.

Angello Network

Angello Network is a global community of visionary leaders and entrepreneurs committed to transforming societies through faith-driven enterprise. Rooted in the principles of connection, collaboration, and communication, the Network seeks to foster entrepreneurial ecosystems that embody integrity, generosity, and Kingdom values.

The journey begins with **gathering** national leaders who carry a vision for their nations. Within trusted circles of faith, learning, and collaboration, these leaders are encouraged to dream boldly, to grow in character and wisdom, and to connect their spiritual calling with practical action. Through these gatherings, Angello Network cultivates a high-trust environment where fellowship, prayer, and shared purpose create the foundation for long-term transformation.

The next stage is to **strengthen** leaders and teams. Through mentoring, peer learning, and tailored training, national leaders gain the tools to translate vision into strategy. They build capable teams, align resources, and develop operational plans that sustain redemptive impact. As leaders grow in faith, competence, and influence, their ecosystems begin to reflect the Kingdom values of generosity, service, and integrity.

Angello Network then works to **empower** these leaders to

build sustainable, Kingdom-driven ecosystems. This involves mobilizing local resources, encouraging collaboration across business, church, and community sectors, and developing pathways for job creation and social mobility. Giving and generosity become engines for local transformation, reducing dependency and fueling new initiatives led by emerging leaders.

Finally, the movement continues to **expand**, as national ecosystems connect across borders. Leaders from diverse regions share knowledge, reinforce one another, and collaborate for collective impact. Through this global fellowship, Angello Network multiplies transformation—linking faith, enterprise, and community renewal across continents.

At its heart, Angello Network believes that business is not merely economic activity but a divine calling to serve, restore, and build. Together, as co-workers with Christ, its members seek to see nations flourish, markets redeemed, and lives transformed for the glory of God.

Angello Innovation Lab

The Angello Innovation Lab is a Global South–based and led imagination-centered think–do tank.

It is a Spirit-led space for discernment, storytelling, and action that helps shape the future of faith-driven enterprise across frontier markets. The Lab is not a fund or a program; it is a container for co-creation where frontier market leaders and global companions work together to reimagine how money, mission, and mutuality can serve Kingdom transformation.

The Lab's purpose is threefold:

- CENTER national visions — by listening to local leaders and extracting catalytic brokering needs and convictions that can accelerate transformation within their countries.
- CULTIVATE partners — by preparing those from the

Global North and South to show up well, as listeners, companions, and co-builders rather than directors of the story.
- CONNECT both sides — through trusted, ethical brokering that translates vision into shared action, learning, and measurable collaboration.

The Lab's rhythm alternates between Tables and Learning Journeys:

Tables are recurring working spaces where frontier-market and global leaders act together on concrete themes such as:

- Inclusive Capital Models – creating locally-led investment pathways that embody dignity and stewardship.
- Showing Up Well in Partnership – building new patterns of collaboration grounded in humility, reciprocity, and accountability.
- Strengthening Local Leadership Networks – mobilising senior mentors and connecting practitioners across nations.

Learning Journeys are locally designed and led immersions where small groups come to listen with their feet and co-design next steps in response to locally felt needs.

Rooted in spiritual discernment and relational trust, the Angello Innovation Lab pioneers a new model of collaboration: one that is Spirit-grounded, imagination-driven, and led from the frontier markets outward.

Chapter Three: Agents For Change

This book is built on conversations with inspiring members of the Angello network, whose stories bring the idea of being an agent for change to life. Each case study grows out of these interviews, capturing the wisdom, struggles, and breakthroughs shared in their own words. These conversations are also featured on the Angello Podcast, available on Spotify and Apple Podcasts.

Fellowship with Malcolm Johnston and Artem Magay

Introduction

Malcolm Johnston is based in Ireland. He is a Partner at Angello and is deeply committed to the Angello network. He has a heart for young people growing up in difficult circumstances and his passion lies in ensuring that the vision of local entrepreneurial leaders is heard, supported, and empowered to create lasting impact. *(See Malcolm's bio in Appendix One).*

Artem Magay was born and raised in the Uzbek Soviet Socialist Republic. In 1991, when Artem was a high school student, the Soviet Union collapsed. With free market opportunities opening up in the newly independent republic of Uzbekistan, Artem opted for a university education in economics and worked in the financial department of an international company before he felt God's call into ministry. As a church pastor in Uzbekistan running charity-oriented projects, Artem was encouraged by Malcolm to think about starting businesses. A turning-point came when Malcolm invited him to a conference in Kenya where Artem realized he needed to change direction. He delegated most of his church work and focused on businesses, discovering them to be *"his life call from God."*

In this insightful interview, Angello network members Malcolm Johnston and Artem Magay share how their relationship came about. They reflect on what it means to integrate Godly principles such as humility, faithfulness, obedience and stewardship into their business operations, relationships and leadership. Their story offers practical guidance and spiritual encouragement for faith-driven leaders walking a similar path from charity projects to fruitful businesses offering job creation and economic stability for poverty-stricken communities. Through their example of passion, resilience and intentional purpose, Malcolm and Artem demonstrate how business can serve as a powerful platform for advancing the kingdom of God, not only in social upliftment but also in the way leaders show up and serve.

Leadership and Impact

Malcolm Johnston and Artem Magay exemplify a style of leadership that is both spiritually grounded and practically effective, marked by ethical integrity, personal transformation and a commitment to impacting others beyond business outcomes. Malcolm brings a boldness rooted in spiritual clarity. His leadership is compassionate; he leads by example, demonstrating what it means to put God first and to trust God with the outcomes. His business approach is spiritual at its core, focused not only on performance metrics but on the transformation of team members, clients, and communities alike.

"The most important thing for me has been to find the discipline to spend time with God … feeding on God's word in the first part of each day meant that what I did was focused on what was eternal rather than what was temporary." – Malcolm.

Artem shows how to remain spiritually sensitive and God-led in difficult political and economic circumstances. His leadership blends strategic vision with a willingness to trust when prompted by God. He models a unique balance between decision-making and discernment.

"For myself, one of the biggest inspirations was recognizing my calling ... understanding that I'm part of something bigger, which is the Kingdom of God." – Artem.

Malcolm met Artem at a Christian conference in Central Asia 17 years ago and immediately identified him as an outstanding young leader with the vision and courage to lead within a difficult context. He was greatly inspired by Artem and continued to keep in touch.

Malcolm recalls that as an entrepreneur in Ireland, he wanted to build a business that would give him the freedom to do other things he was passionate about, such as helping young people who were growing up in difficult circumstances. Following the fall of communism, God sent him to Eastern Europe and Central Asia where there was no business community, very little business activity, and many children and young people in real poverty. The objective was to find local leaders who could be mentored to support these young people. That was when he met Artem and heard about what he was doing and the things he envisioned.

That there should be people in such circumstances with the vision, hope and courage to make a difference inspired Malcolm and became a catalyst for starting Angello. Malcolm's response to God's call on his life was to take to heart and live out, through his business activities and the Angello network, Isaiah 61:1: *"The spirit of the Sovereign Lord is upon me; the Lord has anointed me to preach good news to the poor, bind up the broken-hearted and set the captives free."* He became involved in charity work because it was the only model he knew, and it was while doing charity work in Eastern Europe, helping churches to care about the children in their communities, that he spoke with a Christian leader there about the challenges faced by the churches. He relates how he will never forget him saying, *"That's a great idea, Malcolm, but the people don't stay in the churches because nobody has a job. And if nobody has a job they migrate. The church falls apart."* Malcolm realised there was a much deeper systemic issue to address than providing charity to help the poor. The challenge to him as a businessman was to change his charity mindset.

"Bit by bit, God's challenge to me was, 'You need to think more like a businessperson. If you care about the poor in this calling of Isaiah 61 you need to think about job creation, and what needs to happen so that job creation can happen, because that is so much at the root of stronger churches, stronger Christian community that can impact society.' That was probably the birth of Angello." – Malcolm.

One of Artem's businesses is CrossFit gym, initially established as a place to help children in need. They work with Down-syndrome and autistic children, helping them physically and mentoring them and other young people through the business. Artem describes how young people now ask him for advice, not just as a person who manages finances and has experience in doing business, but as a person who had a call from God and used this call in this direction. Malcolm tells of how, when the CrossFit business had just started, he asked Artem more about it. Artem didn't have a business plan, but he knew his numbers for the business and could describe how, with a little bit of extra investment for equipment to make the gym a nicer place with a bit more capacity, they could increase the membership very easily. Malcolm and his partners provided a loan for the gym, and Malcolm describes how amazing it has been to see how the business has since grown and become a catalyst for other projects.

Malcolm describes CrossFit as a *'lighthouse business'*, with Artem as a *'lighthouse leader'*, a leadership example for those around him in Uzbekistan. What is really exciting for Malcolm is that Artem has begun to identify key entrepreneurial leaders of the next generation. Artem has gathered a group of rising entrepreneurs and is mentoring them and building them as a group.

Artem is humble in his response to Malcolm's praise, explaining the context as that of a post-Soviet generation where most local churches are *"post-Soviet with post-Soviet people."* Nobody ever taught them how to manage finances, or how to do business; for generation after generation, there was no financial literacy. He describes how young people in his church are thirsty for any kind of business training or information because they want to succeed in life. Artem suggested to his church leaders that church should be the place to inspire these young people. As a result, they now offer financial literacy courses through his church, and Artem invites entrepreneurs and professional businesspeople to speak to their youth group on how to start a business, how to make investments from a young age, and how to manage money. Artem sees this as a way to prepare lighthouse leaders.

Artem's personal experience is that his generation has a charity mindset and can't really connect with the multiplication concept. They just think, *"Okay, we are prosperous enough, wealthy enough, we can help by giving."* It's hard to change that mindset. As a result, Artem decided to focus on young people. He was amazed to see how much they can do with a little, and this little starts with words of inspiration, getting them together and telling them, "You can do it. Believe in yourself, because a huge God is behind you. All your resources are given to you by God, for general multiplication and for proclaiming the Kingdom of God." Artem's goal is for these young entrepreneurs to see their businesses as their ministry, where they can glorify God.

"I believe that God has put me at the right time in the right place. Understanding that God has His will in you and put you where you are on purpose, inspires me. You're constantly seeking what you can do for God among your people, that's

where you are, and this really drives me the most." – Artem.

Malcolm and Artem lead with intentionality and presence, believing that real impact begins not with external success but with internal alignment and faithful character. Their leadership has led to tangible, positive changes within not only their organisations but also the communities they impact; changes that reflect Kingdom values in action.

Challenges and Lessons

Malcolm and Artem speak passionately about the challenges and opportunities faced as faith-driven entrepreneurs. Malcolm describes the amazing job Artem did in bringing together the finance through his own efforts, as well as from friends and family, in order to get CrossFit gym off the ground. Malcolm visited the gym, and thought, "*This is amazing, what these guys have achieved.*" Although Artem did not have a business plan, he had all the numbers in his head and built the picture for Malcolm, which had him thinking he could partner with him for the next stage of the business to help it to grow, and to help Artem's confidence.

Artem tells how he lacked self-confidence, thinking that this was not his area of expertise, that he didn't know what he was doing, and that so many people were depending upon him, but he constantly felt Malcolm pushing him forward and challenging him. He has learnt that "when you have all these goals and dreams in your head and you're not sure if they will work or not, or what the next steps should be, to have someone next to you saying, '*Come on, you can do it, this is the way it can work, here is an example,*' is the greatest thing about mentorship."

"It's then that you say to yourself, 'Why not?' And you start to be that businessman, that entrepreneur – to be brave. It's about being brave." – Artem.

Now, Artem is aware of the great opportunity to be a similar mentor to the group of entrepreneurs in Uzbekistan, to see the huge potential in them and say, *'Come on guys, go ahead!'* Artem's words reveal his servant heart, understanding that it is a privilege to know some of them are going to outgrow him, and *"to be a hand of God in their life, to be the one who inspires, to be so good for God, to be His fruit. To serve these people, and to feel for them like they're your children, caring for them and encouraging them."*

"In many emerging markets, the Christian community coming into the marketplace and doing business is very new ... and therefore, like Artem said, many people, even the young people, have never seen examples of what it means to be in business and integrate your faith, not just a business that makes you money for your family, but like Artem said, a business that actually gets involved in multiplication of resources." – Malcolm.

Malcolm has learnt, over time, the importance of being silent before God and *"finding rest on the far side of busy-ness."* God showed him, through pain and things that didn't work out, that learning to be still and enjoying communion with God in silence was just as much preparation for, and part of, the eternal as being busy and active for things that matter. As God led him deeper into this practice, he was shown that he gets to keep forever this enjoyment of communion with God. As an activist, learning to be at rest and to silence his constant thinking has become a huge part of *"investing in the eternal."*

Key Themes and Insights

Several powerful, interconnected themes emerge from the conversation with Malcolm and Artem. These insights reflect how deeply their faith in Christ shapes their entrepreneurial mindset, decisions, and relationships:

Identity in Christ: Both men emphasise that their identity in God is not compartmentalised from their work. It is the foundation for everything they do. Their approach to leadership and business stems directly from this spiritual grounding, influencing how they engage with challenges and opportunities, as well as with their mentees, their clients, and their teams.

"In business there's such a temptation to chase what's temporary, especially wealth and building some kind of status or reputation, and I decided really early on – because I kept coming back to the word of God – to invest in what's eternal. Invest in what's eternal. Invest in what's eternal." – Malcolm.

Spiritual self-discipline and an eternal mind-set: Artem describes how he accepted Jesus as his Saviour at university. This affected his goals and his worldview, connecting him to eternity, not just evaluating life in terms of a human lifespan. This led him into a 'second education' in Theology, following which he returned to Uzbekistan to serve as a church pastor.

"I believe this was one of the most important decisions in my life, to accept Jesus as my personal Saviour, because it affected my lifelong goals and views and everything. So, I kind of re-evaluated what I want to have in the future, because it also connects me to eternity."

Having discerned Isaiah 61:1 as God's call on his life, Malcolm soon discovered that the most important thing to keep him inspired was the discipline to spend time with God and God's word in the first part of each day. Subsequently, Malcolm has learnt that being still, in silence, in the presence of God is a vital component of 'investing in the eternal'.

"I realised that with being in business, and all the pressures around that, if I didn't consume the Mind of God from His word, just from being in silence with him, from being in prayer, if I didn't consume His mindset and what was important to Him and take on board spiritual food before the day got going, then I was going to be pulled in all kinds of directions." – Malcolm.

Faithfulness, humility and the courage to trust: Artem has learnt the value of investing in people and having the courage to trust God for positive outcomes.

"I just trust God, because I understand that without God, I'm small, but we have a great God behind us, so I'm just trying to be faithful ... one of the things is to invest in people. When you plant something in people, this is where your plans start to grow, and you discover people's gifts and talents for God. One of the greatest examples for me in the Bible is John the Baptist, because Jesus calls him the greatest. And all he had was faithfulness. He was faithful. God called him to be in the desert and cry out loud that Jesus is coming. And for faithfulness in this small role, God called him the greatest." – Artem.

Marketplace as Ministry: Malcolm and Artem view the marketplace as a mission field, an extension of their calling. They emphasise that the way you lead, serve and create value should reflect God's nature and bring light into places of influence.

"You think of charity as in 'do good for your neighbours'. But then you come to the point ... okay, there's charity, but how you can really multiply the fruit? Charity is division. In the business world, you're not thinking about addition or division, you're thinking about multiplication. As a businessperson you can increase and multiply the fruit if you use all of your talents and gifts and the resources that you have from the perspective of multiplication." – Artem.

"But when I started thinking of CrossFit as a business for the kingdom, I realized we can also mentor people through the business, and we can reproduce the model of doing this kind of ministry in different areas, in different places." - Artem

"Post communism, Central Asia was a really, really difficult part of the world ... there was no business community ... there were a lot of kids and young people who were in real

poverty and that was what I felt God had called me to. When I met Artem I thought, wow, in the middle of these really difficult circumstances there are people with vision and hope and courage to make a difference and that just immediately inspired me. And I thought if there's anything we can do to help and support people like Artem and these kinds of local leaders, what a privilege!" - Malcolm

Mentorship, Fellowship and Community: Artem reflects on how mentorship has built community, and how walking in fellowship with like-minded believers such as Malcolm has been a source of inspiration, accountability and clarity that he is now able to replicate.

"… one of the big inspirations for me is being amongst the right people. And I think I have not much to do with this, because God blessed me to be surrounded with the great people around me and when you look at them, when you see them being like on fire, doing their passion … the right people who are really, really passionate about their calling." – Artem

"And it seems like God is really using this way, because now I'm 47 I see some other young people, like I was when I met Malcolm, 25, 27 … I see other young people come up to me and ask for advice, not just in doing business, but who has had a call from God, and used this call in this direction." – Artem

Malcolm tells of how Artem's mentorship and leadership in his local community continues to inspire him, twenty years later.

"I think that's absolutely amazing how his vision just keeps widening. And now this investing in these younger entrepreneurs, like high-capacity young entrepreneurs, and he's thinking so strategically about this next generation of people in Uzbekistan, and I think that is super exciting that he acts as their mentor now."

Perseverance and Integrity in the Face of Challenges: Artem refers to the challenges of building business enterprises in the post-Soviet context and how his response was to use the church as a place of education for business practices with Christian values.

"Nobody ever taught us how to manage finances, how to do business, how to start this, how to do start-up, or anything in this way, and most of the people in our communities, generation after generation, there is no financial literacy. That just one day came to the point of, as a church, we should be a leader in this area." – Artem.

"So this is the way, first of all ... a kind of basic level, because through this, I believe this is how we start to prepare the ground for the lighthouses ... Because we should study, and the earlier we start, the better we should discover the gifts." - Artem

Malcolm tells of how Angello started not because they had any idea what to do, but because they could see the way things were being done was not going to get at the root of issues that he saw and really cared about. He credits Artem with teaching him a lot from the context of the challenges faced in the post-Soviet context.

"When I went to visit places like Central Asia, and I just watched and listened to amazing people like Artem ... that inspired me." – Malcolm.

Malcolm highlights the importance of perseverance and holding onto faith through difficulty. His decision-making is guided not by expediency, but by prayer and integrity.

Shared Values as a Platform for Growth: Artem shares that he wouldn't have taken up the challenge without Malcolm's encouragement, and the example of the wider network of companies that integrate Kingdom values into their work has provided opportunities for collaboration and mutual growth. This alignment has helped him to grow professionally and spiritually, connecting strategy with service and innovation with purposeful intentionality.

"Malcolm invited me for this conference in Kenya, Forge. Here I could see all the angels and I should say, this group of people really impacted my heart. Because at that moment, I kind of realised that this is the way I want to do ministry in the future." – Artem.

Malcolm emphasises that the role of value-driven business mentorship in communities by local leaders such as Artem can be a platform for shared vision that goes beyond their own businesses, becoming a catalyst for national and global growth and change.

"There's a huge part now for the church to play in encouraging people that the marketplace is where you can live by being salt and light. There's such a need for great examples and many of the emerging generation are looking around for those examples. One of the most inspiring things is when local businesses run by local people are doing that, and the business becomes … a light to the wider community." - Malcolm.

Malcolm points out that he and his partners in the Angello network are seeing the positive effects of the work of the Angello network in mentoring businesses that integrate spiritual alignment into economic growth.

"We're seeing that across many countries those examples are hugely significant, and the leaders, if they have a vision for their country beyond their business, and if they've dealt with their ego, they've got convening power … and so these Lighthouse businesses are really significant if they're run by these kinds of leaders." – Malcolm.

Key Principles for Faith-Driven Entrepreneurs

Malcolm and Artem share a rich set of principles for entrepreneurs seeking to integrate their faith with their business in a meaningful, sustainable and God-honouring way. These tips reflect both practical wisdom and spiritual depth.

1. Stewardship, Not Ownership

Recognise that your business ultimately belongs to God. Your role is to steward it with care, obedience and accountability — not to control or idolise it. Success is defined by alignment with God's will, not only growth or profit.

2. Build on Kingdom Values

Operate with non-negotiables like integrity, humility, generosity and servant leadership. These values are the bedrock of a God-honouring business. Your business culture reflects your inner life because what you compromise on in private will show up in public. Honesty and consistency in your personal walk will inevitably show up in your organisational culture and relationships.

3. Be Spirit-Led in Strategy

Effective leadership isn't about following formulas; it's about seeking God's direction. Pray over your decisions, listen, and move with discernment rather than ambition or expediency. Be sensitive to God's timing, especially when it means waiting, shifting direction or taking a countercultural step.

4. Seek Wisdom and Community

Don't walk the entrepreneurial journey alone. Surround yourself with people who share your faith, values and vision. Fellowship and accountability are crucial for spiritual clarity, emotional resilience and strategic growth. The Angello network has been a key source of this kind of support for both men.

5. Practice Faith and Perseverance

The road isn't always smooth, but trusting God's plan provides stability in uncertainty. When challenges arise, they are often invitations to lean deeper into God's provision and purpose. Staying the course with faith and perseverance leads to inner growth and long-term fruitfulness.

6. Use Business as a Platform for Service and Impact

Entrepreneurship isn't just about personal success; it's also about creating value that uplifts others. View your business as a means of serving people, building community and advancing the Kingdom of God. Impact is measured not just by what you build, but by how it blesses others.

Reflections on the angello Network and the Acts Community Values

"In many emerging markets, the Christian community coming into the marketplace and doing business is very new … we are at the beginning of a very exciting new movement … many people have never seen examples of what it means to integrate your faith and build a great business, not just a business that makes you money for your family, but like Artem said, a business that actually gets involved in multiplication of resources." – Malcolm.

For Malcolm and Artem, fellowship together with faith-based collaboration is not just theological; it's practical and personally transformative. They describe the Angello model as one of mutual encouragement, trust and accountability, where business leaders are not left to navigate challenges alone but to walk together in intentional relationship. The community shapes not only their business strategies but also their inner lives, encouraging regular check-ins, emotional honesty and a refusal to let professional success substitute for spiritual integrity. The result is a culture where faith and business reinforce each other, and where generosity and service flow naturally from a shared Kingdom vision.

Malcolm and Artem speak with appreciation and clarity about the role Angello has played in their journeys as faith-driven entrepreneurs. At its core, Angello exists to empower entrepreneurs to integrate their faith meaningfully into their business practices, and both leaders believe that goal is being lived out in powerful, tangible ways. Through mentorship, access to resources, and a deeply supportive community, Angello has created an environment where entrepreneurs don't have to choose between faith and business excellence. Instead, they are encouraged to pursue both with integrity and boldness. Malcolm and Artem demonstrate that Angello provides more than networking or professional development; it offers a spiritual ecosystem where faith is not just welcomed but centred.

They describe Angello as a community where believers challenge one another to grow, remain accountable and pursue excellence without compromising their values. For both men, Angello has been a catalyst for both inner and economic growth, a mirror for reflection and a confirmation that faith and business not only intersect, they also belong together.

Future Vision

There's such a need for great examples and many of the emerging generation are looking around for those examples. What does it look like to integrate faith in your business, to be passionate for the kingdom, to learn generosity, to care about your community? What does that look like? I think in our experience one of the most inspiring things that happens is when local businesses run by local people are doing that and become Lighthouse businesses ... that light to the wider community, that's an example and inspiring. And we're seeing that across many countries, in many different places."
– Malcolm.

Malcolm and Artem share a compelling, hope-filled vision for the future in which faith-driven businesses become key agents of societal transformation. They see the Angello network not simply as a fellowship, but as a launchpad for a global community of faith-based business leaders committed to impact, integrity and Kingdom-building purpose.

Looking ahead, both Malcolm and Artem feel strongly called to invest in the next generation of purpose-driven leaders, creating platforms and mentorship spaces that equip young entrepreneurs to lead with character, courage and clarity. For them, raising up others is not a side mission, it is core to the long-term vision of Kingdom entrepreneurship.

Together, they envision a future that is global, creative, disruptive, and also deeply rooted in spiritual discernment. For Malcolm and Artem, the future of Kingdom business will be achieved by faith and obedience to God's call, and will be measured not only merely by growth, visibility and profitability, but by transformation in societal behaviour and mutual collaboration.

"Let's discuss a vision for our country that will bring glory to God …" – Malcolm.

Closing Reflections on the Conversation

The conversation with Malcolm and Artem closes with a powerful reminder: It is entirely possible to be both Spirit-filled and strategy-minded, and to lead with courage while remaining deeply compassionate, pursuing growth without compromising your God-given values.

Their stories are not about perfection, but about intentionality-choosing faithfulness over fame, stewardship over ownership, and character over convenience. They encourage fellow entrepreneurs to stay rooted in trustworthy relationships and lead with mutual respect, and to seek God's voice in every aspect of business. For Malcolm and Artem, success is measured not by accolades or scale, but by obedience, by impact, and by whether their leadership reflects the Kingdom values they profess.

"Meeting Artem was really significant ... to see amazing people like Artem and watch their lives and listen to their story ... was inspiring, to not settle for stupid things that were temporary, but invest in what lasts forever. Because what I saw in Artem was somebody who was doing that at cost, and that was a real push to me, to not settle for less important things." – Malcolm.

"You see, if the glove is just hanging, it's just empty. However, if you put the hand inside the glove, it starts working. So, for myself, this is the great example of my life, because if you have God in you, and if you're driven by God, by His purpose, by His Spirit, and you understand His calling, that you are called again and again to play your part in this generation." – Artem.

Discipleship with Paul Lindsay and Roy Crowne

Introduction

In a compelling conversation, Paul Lindsay and Roy Crowne, both prominent members of the Angello network, share their journeys as faith-driven entrepreneurs and leaders. Drawing on rich experiences from construction sites of London, marketplaces in Nairobi, and mission trips to Moscow, they explore the powerful relationship between Godly principles and business. Through stories marked by struggle, divine guidance and radical generosity, Paul and Roy illustrate how faith shapes not only business operations and leadership but also relationships and community impact. Their reflections offer practical wisdom and encouragement for entrepreneurs in fellowship, showing that when anchored in Biblical values, enterprise becomes a transformative force for good in the world.

Paul Lindsay is a seasoned construction industry professional with over thirty-five years of experience working with FTSE100 companies across various sectors in London. He is a fellow of the Royal Institution of Chartered Surveyors, a trustee of Angello Development Foundation and the chair of the board for Youth for Christ (YFC) Moscow Region, Russia. (*See Paul's bio in Appendix One*).

In his leadership role at ADF, Paul is committed to supporting the Foundation's mission by providing a platform for influence, deploying director time, making grants and supporting catalytic investments. The Foundation's work is to engage with the socially disadvantaged and promote the justice integral to God's gospel, thereby advancing God's Kingdom. ADF's approach to mission, rooted in the experience of working with charities in Belfast and Eastern Europe, led them to embrace Entrepreneurial Leadership Development (ELD) as a tool for empowering faith and society by helping individuals and communities achieve self-sufficiency.

Paul's convictions are centred on the values expressed in Micah 6:8: "Do justice, love mercy, walk humbly." He is passionate about driving faith-driven change through thought leadership and influence, modelling the Angello Theory of Change, and embracing a radical community approach that emphasises fellowship, generosity, service, impact and joy. As a catalytic faith agency, ADF is dedicated to advancing God's Kingdom through practical, transformative work locally and globally.

Roy Crowne grew up with no church background in the East End of London, a Cockney with a natural affinity for enterprise, for whom faith would eventually become the compass for his life and work. As a young boy, he spent hours at his grandfather's market stall, selling fruit and vegetables, learning early lessons in negotiation and resilience. "There's a buzz … something about getting a deal, offering a deal, that just gave me excitement," he recalls. These early experiences sparked a love for entrepreneurship and taught him the value of initiative and self-reliance.

At school, Roy met a Christian peer who challenged him to consider the claims of Jesus. This encounter led to a transformative experience at a residential Christian camp where he committed his life to Christ at the age of sixteen. That moment, which he describes as both "scary" and "supernatural," marked the beginning of a profound transformation, experiencing God's presence in a deeply personal way. This "vertical relationship," he notes, "changed every other relationship" and gave him a newfound purpose and eternal perspective on life. Within two weeks, he had read the entire Bible, immersing himself in Scripture and discovering a sense of mission that would guide all his future endeavours.

This early foundation of faith and purpose guided Roy through studies in theology, entrepreneurial ventures in car sales, and ultimately leadership roles in Youth for Christ (YFC) United Kingdom, the last 13 years as National Director. Roy was a co-founder of Hope 08 and served as Executive Director of HOPE, bringing churches together for the purpose of mission. In 2021 he launched Gospel Entrepreneurs. (*See Roy's bio in Appendix One*).

Leadership and Impact

When Paul was 19, he spent a year as a missionary in Khartoum, Sudan, a season that proved hugely influential for his faith. After that year, Paul recalls sitting in London's Victoria Station waiting to return to his home in Belfast, considering whether he really wanted to be a missionary or whether he should stay in London and take up a place offered to him at Thames Polytechnic in London to study surveying. He sensed very clearly that God wanted him to complete the four years of study in London, and he realised "*there are lots of ways to be a missionary, even though you're working.*"

After qualifying, Paul worked in several jobs before teaming up with a friend to start a construction business. Paul had no experience or family background in business. His father worked in the Belfast shipyards; his mother cleaned university halls of residence. The first contract was with a local co-op — modest beginnings, but Paul knew God was in it, and he sensed that if they were going to make the business work, he would have to commit time to meeting with God, because "God does know how to work business and … what all the bits do." Paul committed to meeting with God every morning at 6 a.m. to listen for direction. That quiet discipline became his anchor, shaping not just how he made decisions, but how he led, built relationships, and navigated the pressures of the business world. It was a rhythm that carried him from those first projects to becoming a partner in a construction consultancy and then an independent consultant, working and living missionally, including serving and leading YFC in Moscow and Russia.

Roy Crowne's commitment to his faith at an early age quickly translated into action. He asked his headmaster for permission to lead a school assembly in which he shared his testimony with 1,000 pupils, learning that speaking publicly about his beliefs leads to action. This early act of courage laid the foundation for a lifetime of leadership and influence. He later went on to study theology and discern his calling, recognizing the importance of directing his entrepreneurial instincts and spiritual purpose into evangelical leadership. A defining moment observing ponies in the New Forest reinforced this clarity; Roy felt God directing him as Samuel challenged Saul: "Don't waste your life chasing donkeys. Do what you've been called to do." This conviction shaped his vocational path, leading him into leadership roles in YFC UK, and partnering with Paul Lindsay within the Angello network.

Roy also highlights the pivotal role of mentorship in navigating the intersection of faith and leadership. Early in his ministry he connected with Sir Michael Coleman, a seasoned businessman who coached him in business acumen and helped him navigate the practical challenges of running a ministry. These lessons reinforced the importance of guidance, accountability, and learning from experienced leaders.

Reflecting on his journey, Roy notes that every formative experience, from the market stall to mentorship, from committing to Christ to stepping into leadership taught him that faith, courage and relational support are inseparable from effective leadership and entrepreneurial impact. Each challenge and opportunity contributed to resilience, discernment, and the ability to serve others faithfully in both ministry and business.

Paul credits fellow Irishman Malcolm Johnson, whom he met when he had just come to faith at the age of 15, with persuading him to "stay on the narrow road", even when he went to London and "tried to get away from him." Malcom "kept after him", pushing a global view and "a sense of the bigger picture." Paul's year in Sudan had formed good habits and a thirst for more; the challenge that lay before him was how to integrate his desire to work in business and be a witness. Paul's involvement in Youth for Christ in Eastern Europe came about in 2002 when Malcolm invited Paul to Moldova. Malcom had become the Eastern European Director for YFC, and Paul tells of how, on the flight back, Malcom had asked, "*You fancy doing something like this?*" Paul replied, "*Yeah, of course … I've just got like, three kids and a wife and a mortgage and a new business. But, yeah, hey, why not?*" In 2004 Malcolm called and said, "*You fancy going to Moscow?*" Paul's response was, "*Yeah, sign me up.*" Paul is now the Chair of the board for YFC Moscow Region, Russia.

For Paul and Roy, leadership is not defined by titles or roles but by surrendered availability – the willingness to follow God's call and be present where needed. Their leadership is further shaped by practical engagement and a willingness to step into challenging contexts. In launching his own construction business with no prior experience, Paul had to navigate uncertainty, manage practical logistics, and build a team from scratch. He credits daily time with God as essential to making decisions and persevering through the pressures of starting a business, showing that effective leadership is both practical and spiritually anchored. Roy's formative experiences in London markets and early entrepreneurial ventures highlight the importance of initiative and adaptability. By learning to trade fruit and vegetables at his grandfather's market stall he developed an early sense of responsibility, negotiation, and engagement with diverse people - skills that would later underpin his leadership in ministry and business.

The work of both men reveals the power of courageous conviction, whether that be in venturing into unfamiliar countries or launching bold initiatives. They are deeply committed to leading in ways that bring about personal and societal transformation. Through both business and ministry, their work has positively impacted employees, customers, churches, youth and entire communities. Paul's leadership in building YFC teams across Eastern Europe and Roy's efforts to bring the gospel into public life through Hope 08 and YFC UK are powerful examples of this impact. Their conviction has been essential to Kingdom growth, creating a multiplying effect way beyond their own influence. Their leadership embraces diversity and emphasizes relational depth that extends far beyond borders. Paul's hands-on involvement in Russia and Moscow and Roy's international partnerships show how cross-cultural collaboration can strengthen the Church and expand impact.

A hallmark of their leadership is intentional mentorship and relational engagement, as seen in their passion for mentoring younger leaders and entrepreneurs. Paul intentionally invests in local leaders across Eastern Europe, equipping them to lead YFC initiatives, while Roy translates spiritual conviction into practical guidance for others. Their commitment to nurturing others creates a multiplying effect that extends far beyond their personal influence. Both men's leadership embraces global engagement, diversity, and relational depth, showing that effective Kingdom impact combines strategic thinking with care, encouragement, and hands-on support. Roy expresses his admiration for Paul's global vision and recalls that his relationship with Paul began when Paul invited him to come to Russia and help him with Rock Solid, a YFC youth programme in Moscow.

"It was a unique experience, let me tell you, but it was fantastic, and it built an amazing relationship that's gone on and on and on, and I love him to bits". – Roy.

The conversation with Paul and Roy illustrates a leadership style developed through formative experiences and disciplined practices. Paul emphasizes the daily discipline of rising early to meet with God to stay present and responsive to the needs around him, ensuring that leadership decisions are prayerfully grounded. Roy's act of speaking at his school assembly shortly after committing his life to Christ as a teenager demonstrates courage, initiative, and a willingness to step into public leadership, despite having no prior experience. These moments reveal a consistent pattern: Both men seize real-world opportunities to lead faithfully in real-world contexts, modelling conviction, courage, humility, and relational depth.

"Why can't we engage with those who aren't of our culture and do things with them? Because our faith is transcendent of our culture, our nationality, our ethnicity ... your experience of God is only going to get richer the more people you bump into who don't think like you, but who still have faith." – Paul.

Challenges and Lessons

Paul and Roy openly acknowledge the inherent uncertainty in business and ministry, especially when operating across diverse international contexts like Uzbekistan, Kenya, Russia, and Moldova.

Paul recalls arriving in Khartoum from Belfast at age 19, navigating a completely unfamiliar environment while reflecting on his calling, and later stepping into construction and consultancy projects in London with no prior business experience. These early experiences taught him that preparation alone is not enough; faith and discernment are essential for navigating the unknown. Similarly, Roy reflects on running Youth for Christ programs in the UK and internationally, noting that managing a ministry is not unlike running a business - budgets are tight, trust must be earned, and unexpected obstacles are constant.

In these environments, access to capital is limited, financial systems are tightly regulated, and cultural barriers to trust are significant. In the face of these challenges, both men emphasize the critical importance of staying grounded in faith amid complexity. For them, prayer, discernment and dependence on God are essential tools in navigating complexity. For Paul, rising early each day for prayer and reflection during the start-up phase of his business enabled him to make decisions prayerfully, manage stress, and remain responsive to challenges. Similarly, Roy, after drawing on his teenage experience of how publicly sharing his faith in a school assembly impacted his life, illustrates how courage, obedience, and spiritual resilience strengthen practical leadership.

"I then realized that once you go public about your faith, everything changes. And the Bible says, doesn't it, 'Believe in your heart, but confess with your mouth.' You can believe in your heart, but when you confess it, speak it out, things change." – Roy.

Not every investment or initiative has succeeded. Paul candidly recalls ventures in construction and consultancy that fell short of expectations, viewing them as opportunities to refine character, sharpen decision-making, and deepen reliance on God. Similarly, Roy recounts that when he became national director of YFC it was at a low ebb, with multiple challenges. He needed a mentor to help him with business *"because running a ministry is not dissimilar to run a business, particularly when it's struggling."* That was when mentorship from Sir Michael Coleman provided practical guidance in organizational strategy and business acumen. These experiences underscore the transformative power of relational leadership and coaching in navigating challenges. Both men reflectively view setbacks not as failures, but as opportunities for growth – moments that refine character, sharpen decision-making and deepen their reliance on God's guidance.

One of the central lessons Paul and Roy highlight is the importance of marrying generosity with wisdom. In contexts where financial trust is fragile, whether in business or ministry, the need for careful evaluation, ethical stewardship and long-term relationship-building becomes even more important. As a trustee of the Angello Development Foundation, Paul emphasizes that although entrepreneurship involves risk-taking, generosity without discernment and asking searching questions can be ineffective. Roy demonstrates this principle while mentoring young leaders on international programmes, ensuring both their spiritual and operational growth.

"We do get into spaces where things don't go well and money doesn't come back, and we've had to take some of that on the chin and realize that perhaps that wasn't the best investment, and maybe we need to learn things." – Paul.

In all of this, the experiences of Paul and Roy reveal deep resilience, shaped not only by repeated exposure to uncertainty but also by their conviction and a consistent commitment to act faithfully, responsibly, and boldly.

"We don't know all the answers, but we're happy in that with God's guidance, we can make a difference." – Paul.

Key Themes and Insights

Faith as the Foundation for Business and Life: At the heart of the entrepreneurial journeys of both Paul and Roy lies a deep, personal relationship with God. They stress that success in business begins with spiritual alignment, starting each day with intentional time spent with God and seeking His guidance in decision-making.

"If I was going to make a success of it, I definitely had to invite Him into the picture." – Paul.

"This vertical relationship changed every other relationship." – Roy.

Business as a Calling, not just a Career: For Paul, starting a business without prior experience was not a career move but a response to a clear prompting from God. Similarly, Roy transitioned from engineering and car sales to ministry and entrepreneurship, discovering that purpose and passion align when faith leads the way.

"Lots of folks miss God's plan for their life because they don't press into what's in front of them. They don't press into what's the immediate thing to do. If you press into that and take God at His Word, then who knows where it's going to lead? That

means you need to spend more time with Him, because you have got to hear what God's saying, and you won't get to hear what God's saying unless you spend time with Him. And so, for me, it's all about, how tight are you with God? Can you hear His voice? You have got to recognize, yes, that really is the Almighty in me. You know, it's a bit like Samuel ... God's talking to him, and he can't work it out. Hang on, hang on. And then suddenly, yeah, that's the Lord." – Paul.

"I think God's plan is, 'What do you like to do? What excites you? What gives you energy? What gives you drive?' God's Spirit is in who we are, saying, 'Well, have a go, step out.' I think we often spell faith as r-i-s-k. I don't think it's risk. Faith is just doing what you're told" - Roy.

Mission in the Marketplace: Roy's early love for the market and Paul's construction background both evolved into missional expressions of faith. Their stories challenge the divide between sacred and secular, showing that entrepreneurship can be a meaningful form of ministry.

"I want to release the entrepreneurial gift in the local church because I think the local church has struggled to affirm the entrepreneur ... they do know to ask for their money, but they don't know what to do with them. So, what I've now discovered is that the entrepreneurial gift is a gift from God. I would say it's a bit apostolic ... we're releasing that gift and saying, "God affirms you in it, here's a mentor to release you, and listen." – Roy.

Reimagining Missions from 'To' to 'With': Paul and Roy advocate a new model of mission, one that empowers local leaders and entrepreneurs through mentorship and investment, rather than delivering top-down aid.

"Historically, missionaries have had the mindset, "I'm coming to do this 'for' you.' We say, 'We're coming to do this 'with' you." And the 'with' is ... I'm just going to be a critical friend. That's a very different model." – Roy

Community, Fellowship and Shared Purpose: The Angello network and broader faith-based partnerships are vital sources of encouragement, accountability and collective wisdom. Paul and Roy emphasise the value of being surrounded by like-minded believers who can speak truth, share resources, and walk the journey together.

"What the Foundation wants to do is to invest in businesses and enterprises that we believe have got a future in terms of job creation … we have collaborated with other like-minded foundations or faith groups who impact and support those who have a faith and believe that God has given them an amazing gift and that those gifts are completely aligned with His good grace." – Paul.

Resilience and Perseverance through Faith: Both men have faced significant challenges, from financial uncertainty to cultural barriers; but faith, prayer, and a long-term view anchored in God's promises have been the foundations for perseverance. In this way, they remind fellow entrepreneurs that transformation is often forged in adversity.

"If it all goes terribly wrong, even that's not a problem; it will give you a great memory and you'll learn some good lessons, because we've all been there. But learn what you need to learn and go again - that whole 'launch and learn as you go' is the entrepreneurial spirit. And the other thing I found about entrepreneurs, which is why I love being around them, is risk. Risk is the river they swim in. That's what gets them up in the morning. It's like, this is fun, whereas to most people, it's like, 'Uh …' they're like, 'No.' And I think for too long, we've suppressed that gift within the Church of Jesus Christ. Part of what I'm trying to do is release it, affirm it, and just let it go." – Roy.

Key Principles for Faith-Driven Entrepreneurs

1. Start where you are: Obedience over Optics

Paul points out that we're all born somewhere and have connections, a network. Explore where that can take you. God has given us an intellect and the Holy Spirit, so we should be able to use both of those to work out a plan. Many people delay taking action, waiting for the perfect opportunity or big calling. Paul emphasizes the importance of pressing into what's directly in front of you with faith and obedience. Even small beginnings can lead to great impact when aligned with God's purpose.

"Lots of folks can miss it because they don't press into what's in front of them." – Paul.

Roy urges a faith-filled response to the creative energy provided by the Holy Spirit.

"What excites you? What gives you energy? What gives you drive? God's Spirit is in who we are, saying, 'Well, have a go, step out.'" – Roy.

2. Cultivate Daily Devotion to Fuel Direction

Consistent time with God provides clarity and the wisdom needed for leadership and tough business decisions. Early in his career Paul began rising early to prioritise this time. Hearing from God regularly builds spiritual resilience and sharpens discernment.

"God does know how to work business...if I was going to make a success of it, I definitely had to help Him into the picture." – Paul.

3. Understand the Difference between Risk and Faith

Roy challenges the common association of faith with reckless risk-taking. Instead, true faith is about obedience — doing what God calls you to do, which may seem "risky" but really isn't, if you practise St. Paul's advice in Ephesians Ch. 5.

"We often spell faith as r-i-s-k. I don't think it's risk. Faith is just doing what you're told…All that is in Ephesians 5 makes for an effective business. If you haven't got it all, then you aren't going to thrive." – Roy.

4. Affirm and Embrace the Entrepreneurial Gift

Entrepreneurship is often misunderstood or underappreciated in faith communities. Roy highlights it as a spiritual gift akin to an apostolic role, bringing innovation and expansion to the Kingdom. Recognizing and affirming this gift is crucial for individuals and the broader Church.

"The entrepreneurial gift is a gift from God…a bit apostolic." – Roy.

5. Lead with Integrity and Honesty

Paul and Roy emphasize that transparency, ethics and consistency are non-negotiable in all dealings. These values honour God and build long-term trust with clients, partners and teams.

"At the Angello Development Foundation we have interesting conversations with the bank. Why are you sending money to Uzbekistan? Will it come back? Are you sure you're not money laundering? Are you sure that it's risk free? And obviously, we know it's not risk free, so that opens up conversations…it sounds like you're some kind of loan shark lending out money to people that you've never met, and who are the people who've given you the money? It always gives a great lead into just talking about faith, because suddenly there's no barriers. When people say,' Why are you doing this crazy stuff?' and we say, 'Well, it's all because of a faith,' they're very interested. 'You must have real faith, because you're actually giving

money to people that may never come back.' – Paul.

"Jesus wanted to explain that your money is just a tool; either use it well, or if you use it poorly it dominates you. So therefore, learn how to work it out, learn how it works and how the world works ..." – Roy.

6. Practise Servant Leadership and Humility in Relationships

True leadership is about serving others, not elevating oneself. By leading with humility, care and empathy, entrepreneurs create healthier work environments and stronger team dynamics.

"I experienced something supernatural. I was talking in in a way that I'm talking to you now, but as I was talking, the Spirit was doing something in my life, and I became emotional. I knelt, because that seemed the appropriate thing to do, and I experienced the presence of God. That changed everything ... the relationship with God then changed my relationship with my parents. It changed my relationship with the head teacher in my school. This vertical relationship changed every other relationship." – Roy.

7. Set Purpose-Driven Goals Aligned with Faith

Business success isn't just about profits, it's about purpose. It's about dignity, opportunity, and long-term community transformation.

"Spend more time getting to know God, because then you'll get the answer to 'Where should I go?'" – Paul.

Reflections on the Angello Network and the Acts Community Values

Both Paul and Roy are actively involved in the Angello Development Foundation (ADF). Paul describes the heart of the Foundation as recognizing and supporting God-given gifts in others:

"They see that those gifts they've got are completely aligned with His good grace." – Paul.

At the heart of the Angello network is a commitment to relational connection rooted in shared faith. Members are encouraged to connect, collaborate, and support one another in their entrepreneurial and missional pursuits. Rather than a traditional donor-recipient dynamic, Angello promotes partnership, co-labouring with local leaders and entrepreneurs to create contextually relevant, sustainable impact.

Roy and Paul emphasize the importance of building a network that listens, empowers and co-creates. Their approach stands in contrast to older mission models that focused on "doing to" rather than "doing with." They discuss stewardship of resources, faith-infused approaches to money, and responsible management for Kingdom purposes.

Angello's faith-based networking invites mutual respect, shared learning, and ongoing spiritual encouragement, united by core values such as compassion, generosity, trust and responsible stewardship. These values actively inform investment strategies, business operations and interpersonal dynamics.

Roy challenges others to reflect on their relationship with money, using a provocative question:

"If money was a person and ... he or she came in the room, how would you react?"

The Angello Development Foundation seeks to create a culture where money is not idolized or feared but, rather, stewarded wisely in the service of Kingdom impact. This spiritually relational attitude towards wealth, risk and generosity can positively influence how entrepreneurs operate. The Foundation is more than an impact fund; it is a faith-infused ecosystem that re-imagines how believers can steward capital, skills and vision for Kingdom purposes. As both Paul Lindsay and Roy Crowne reflect, Angello serves as a catalytic network and faith community committed to integrating spiritual values into business practice while creating tangible, lasting impact in communities around the world.

"If we're going to change how folks live in other countries, we need to create jobs." – Paul.

Angello's goals are firmly aligned with its mission to bring faith into the heart of business. Paul and Roy view their work through this lens of calling, seeing entrepreneurship not as a sphere separate from ministry, but as a continuation of it. They highlight the importance of investing in ventures that uphold dignity, foster opportunity and embody Christ-centred leadership.

Future Vision

Looking ahead, Paul and Roy are committed to broadening the reach of the Angello network by engaging more faith-driven entrepreneurs and expanding into new regions and sectors. Their vision is not simply about growth for its own sake, but about creating deeper, lasting impact—empowering communities through job creation, mentorship and spiritually grounded enterprise.

"The core of the foundation is that in countries where money and finance is tightly controlled or not accessible, ideas can't thrive or progress because of lack of money and the ongoing climate ... what the Foundation wants to do is to take an amount of money and to invest that in businesses and enterprises that we believe have got a future, and have got a future in terms of job creation." – Paul.

They are especially passionate about releasing the potential of emerging leaders, A key component of their vision involves equipping the next generation of gospel-influenced entrepreneurs. Roy's Gospel Entrepreneurs initiative is focused on building intergenerational bridges by connecting seasoned businesspeople with younger entrepreneurs who need guidance, encouragement and affirmation, developing them to take a strong Christian lead in church, ministry and business. Both Paul and Roy see such transfer of wisdom as central to long-term Kingdom impact.

"They want to give what they've learned as an entrepreneur to another entrepreneur. But they don't know the vehicle. I'm providing the vehicle" – Roy.

These examples illustrate the Angello network's focus on combining financial support with practical guidance and ongoing mentorship, equipping emerging entrepreneurs to grow sustainably and make tangible Kingdom impact.

Ultimately, their dream is to see a thriving global ecosystem of unapologetically faith-driven entrepreneurs who are doing business differently, stewarding resources responsibly, and bringing the values of the Kingdom into the heart of the marketplace. Through Angello and its growing network, they hope to model and multiply a way of working that puts people over profit and purpose above prestige.

Closing Reflections on the Conversation

This conversation with Paul Lindsay and Roy Crowne stands as a masterclass in integrating faith and business. It is rich in wisdom, rooted in humility, and full of practical guidance for anyone seeking to bring to fruition their calling as a faith-driven entrepreneur. Their reflections offer more than insight: They offer inspiration and a challenge to live with purpose, integrity and a Kingdom perspective.

Both Paul and Roy express deep gratitude for the fellowship, mentorship and support found within the Angello network. They are hopeful for the future, not because the path is easy but because they have seen what God can do through a person's obedience, collaboration, and courage. Their confidence lies not in systems or strategy alone, but in a faith that continues to guide their vision and decisions.

"God says, 'Come into the field … now what do you dream about?'" – Roy.

Their stories serve as a powerful invitation to others in business and ministry to:

- Live out your faith boldly in the marketplace.
- Invest in relationships that stretch, challenge and grow you.
- See money not as a threat or idol, but as a tool for Kingdom work.
- Start now — right where you are — and trust God with the outcome.

"You must have real faith, because you're giving money that may never come back" – Paul.

In a world often marked by competition and scarcity, Paul and Roy offer a vision of business shaped by abundance, trust and spiritual conviction. Their lives bear witness to the truth that faith is not a separate track from business; it is the foundation on which truly transformative enterprise is built.

Hospitality with Ralph Catto, Luvuyo Rani and Colin Habberton

Introduction

Luvuyo Rani is the Founder and CEO of Silulo Ulutho Technologies, a pioneering social enterprise bridging the digital divide across South Africa. (*See Luvuyo's bio in Appendix One*)

Since launching Silulo in 2004 selling refurbished computers from the boot of a car, Luvuyo has grown the company to 42 branches across the Western Cape, Eastern Cape, and KwaZulu-Natal. Silulo now provides business services, mobile repairs, B2B solutions, and digital skills training, with a strong presence in underserved townships and rural communities. Luvuyo drives the company's overall strategy while overseeing public relations and stakeholder engagement. Under his leadership, Silulo is advancing system integration and data-driven alignment through CRM and backend innovations.

At the time of its founding, Silulo operated in a township environment marked by limited infrastructure, scarce capital, and systemic barriers for Black entrepreneurs. These conditions not only created urgent social needs but also demanded the entrepreneurial grit, resilience and creativity that would become central to Silulo's culture. Luvuyo's approach combined a commitment to community impact with innovative business solutions, setting the foundation for a model that prioritizes both social transformation and sustainable enterprise growth.

Ralph Catto is a Scottish entrepreneur and investor with a deep commitment to blending social impact with commercial strategy. He began his career in corporate finance at a London stockbroking firm before following his passion for social change by founding a software start-up focused on social housing. This move reflected his dedication to leveraging business as a force for good, addressing social needs through sustainable enterprise. (*See Ralph's bio in Appendix One*)

As a member of the Angello Network, Ralph actively invests in businesses that generate meaningful social impact. He has served as a trustee of the Transformational Business Network (TBN), a Christian, non-discriminatory organization that empowers enterprises in developing countries to lift communities out of poverty. His work has taken him to Africa and the Balkans, while also serving as a trustee for local charities and supporting church operations behind the scenes. Ralph consistently combines financial diligence with relational trust, understanding that early-stage ventures in emerging markets require both capital and the patience to navigate local realities.

Colin Habberton is the Co-Founder and Executive Director of the Relativ Group, an impact solutions provider based in Cape Town, South Africa, with subsidiaries in Canada and New Zealand. (*See Colin's Bio in Appendix One*)

Colin is the interviewer in the Angello podcasts captured in this publication. In the conversation with Ralph and Luvuyo, Colin serves not only as facilitator but also as a key protagonist in the story. As a founding voice in TBN and a long-time collaborator with both Ralph and Luvuyo, Colin played a pivotal role in the early investment in Silulo and helped to facilitate the relational, strategic and financial foundations of their journey. His perspective as both impact practitioner and community builder adds depth to this shared narrative.

In this conversation, Luvuyo, Ralph and Colin reflect on their shared journey of faith and purpose-driven entrepreneurship. What began as an improbable investment in an insolvent internet café in Khayelitsha grew into an extremely successful initiative and a calling that transforms lives, businesses, and communities. It also led to deep friendship between the three men.

Their conversation explores the pivotal moments that shaped their work, and the enduring influence of Godly principles such as humility, servant leadership, and investment in people, not only as spiritual values but also as deeply practical business strategies. Through stories of risk, resilience and radical relationship they offer a compelling blueprint for building enterprises that blend profit with purpose and prioritise human dignity.

"If you want to be successful in business, whether you've got faith or not just switch on to the idea of the New Testament. Read it as a leadership book and you'll win." – Ralph

Leadership and Impact

The leadership styles of all three men converge around one core idea: People come first. Here, the emphasis is that business success is secondary to the transformation of lives. This is reflected in their leadership philosophies.

Ralph, a self-described capitalist who "bleeds capitalism," merges business acumen with Christian conviction as he allows his faith to temper strategy with service. He speaks openly about the effectiveness of servant leadership, placing others ahead of oneself. His leadership is shaped by humility, listening, and letting others shine.

"Dr. Kim Tan had seen Luvuyo already and had recommended him as someone to see. And I've got a picture in front of me of the shop that we went to see … it was a kind of a training environment, and it was slightly organized chaos, and I remember thinking, I don't really know what to make of this. But in the in the middle of the shop, was an upside-down photocopy box. I looked in the box and picked up a handwritten CV, and then another … under that, another handwritten CV. Hang on, wait, what is this? 'Well,' says Luvuyo, 'these are people applying for jobs in Cape Town, because this is in one of the townships, and they've got to do it via email. They haven't got an email. They don't know

necessarily how to type. So we apply for the job for them.' And I just sat there and thought ... this little shop is creating hundreds and hundreds of jobs, potentially, in an area which really needs jobs. You know, if you want to get on in life, put people first. And seeing Luvuyo's passion for the people gave us a tiny little glimpse of what was going on in that organization ... at that point, I thought, I'm in." – Ralph.

Colin brings a systems-oriented perspective, designing environments where others, particularly those historically excluded, can thrive. In his work he focuses on building sustainable ecosystems that weave together relationships, capital, and operational strategy, ensuring that growth and impact are resilient, scalable, and designed to endure beyond individual leadership.

"...the investment was in the region of about 20,000 Pounds. 500,000 Rand at that particular point in time. but there was also a relationship that extended across the time that the capital was invested ... it was a loan, so there was a degree of trust connected to that. And it was paid back in full well within the time that was expected." – Colin.

Luvuyo's leadership is rooted in service, humility, and empowerment. His journey from entrepreneur to mentor and ecosystem builder exemplifies the principle of raising up others, turning leadership into legacy. A key manifestation of this is Silulo's evolution into a franchise model, deliberately designed to enable former employees to move beyond traditional staff roles and become business owners. This approach aimed to not only equip them with entrepreneurial skills and financial independence, but also to ensure that economic opportunity, decision-making power, and leadership capacity remain within the township communities. By embedding ownership locally, Silulo cultivates a culture where wealth creation and strategic influence circulate within the communities it serves, reinforcing both lasting social impact and sustainable growth.

"I could now see the value of TBN individuals, that before an

investment, it is about people connecting, and that connection is still a connection that we have today, even after 10 years of not seeing each other, because now we have that kind of love, understanding and the deep connection." – Luvuyo.

Luvuyo tells of how, following TBN's belief in him, he realised that in life everyone needs someone who believes in them. Silulo became a social franchise, giving staff members an opportunity to buy a franchise. Luvuyo found different funders to support them, and in some cases Silulo stood surety. They were not all successful and some stores and franchises were closed. Others are now investing in properties, transport and diverse businesses, and are growing. UCT now uses Silulo as a case study in the MBA course on how to scale a social franchise, using the lessons Silulo learned.

Luvuyo is no longer involved in Silulo. He now works with Africa Forward, a movement of social entrepreneurs who believe social entrepreneurship is the future for the continent. He takes a lead in policy development and is advising the government on policies for the funding and support of entrepreneurs. He is also advising the G20 on how to position social entrepreneurship in the townships. Further, he has started a Foundation to give back to the community where he started, growing other entrepreneurs.

"Today, we're starting a fifth cohort. I'm not there, and it's growing without me. That for me gives me joy."- Luvuyo.

Challenges and Lessons

Luvuyo confronted systemic exclusion and built his business against the odds. Ralph had to learn cross-cultural humility in investing. Colin, as the bridge between worlds, held the tension between vision and viability, facilitating early funding while nurturing long-term trust.

"Relational capital is often the most catalytic capital." – Colin.
Luvuyo began Silulo operating out of a garage, with no access

to capital after being blacklisted by banks. Yet he persisted, building the business from the ground up. His greatest challenge was not just securing financing but navigating the systemic barriers faced by many Black entrepreneurs in South Africa. Banks denied him credit, suppliers were hesitant to extend terms, and digital infrastructure in township areas was often unreliable. Each obstacle demanded creative problem-solving and relentless relationship-building. Every rejection became an opportunity to cultivate humility, resourcefulness, and an unwavering commitment to meeting the needs of the community.

"Most Black entrepreneurs have amazing ideas but no seed capital. And without someone to believe in them, they can't scale." – Luvuyo

Ralph's challenge was different. Working with UK-based investors accustomed to quick returns required him to cultivate patience and demonstrate the value of listening, even when metrics and spreadsheets demanded faster action. He often had to guide these investors to approach cross-cultural investment with humility, emphasizing understanding before making any decisions:

"I used to take businesspeople from the UK and basically sit them down at Heathrow and say, 'Two ears and one mouth, use them in that ratio, because you do not understand these cultures. And if you ever say something like … in the UK, we do it this way … just shut up, because you don't understand it. And let's not pretend that we are better than them. We're not.'" – Ralph.

Ralph self-deprecatingly admits that when it comes to business, he is not very clever and not very academic, but he seems to work harder than most people and maybe has more common sense. One of his most profound revelations came when working in the Balkans. He was privileged to be invited to the second annual post-war prayer breakfast in Albania. He remembers asking the organizer:

"What on Earth? How are we going to handle all these disparate views ... people who were fighting a couple of years ago, Muslims, Orthodox, Christians, Catholics, Protestants ... How does this work?" And he said, "We use the model of Jesus." "What do you mean by that?" I asked. And he says, "Well, we use the leadership model of Jesus, because actually, we can all agree that he's an important person in history ... we just focus on him as a leadership model."

After that, Ralph began to think much more deeply about leadership. He tells of reading something out of the Harvard Business Review about 'level five leadership.' Level five leaders outperform everyone else but put themselves last. They put others first. He realized that to use the Jesus leadership model in any context was a massive advantage. He also realized that to lead, you have to have a team, and if you're constantly putting your team first, it's much more effective.

"To facilitate effectively, make yourself redundant That is servant leadership. That is Jesus leadership ... If you want to be successful in business, whether you've got faith or not, just switch on to the idea of the New Testament. Read it as a leadership book, and you'll win." – Ralph.

Luvuyo agrees with this and encourages people to switch on the idea of the New Testament as a leadership book. He relates that he learnt resilience from his mother who was arrested during the apartheid years for running a shebeen, but she came back and provided for her family and others and both she and Luvuyo were saved ... they were struggling and in deep poverty, but at home, *"it was love and Jesus will provide. And so we had faith that things will be better, and it's a faith that my mother gave me."* There was a year when Luvuyo could not attend university because there was no money; he explains that while sitting in a township with limited prospects it is easy to lose self-esteem and fall into depression, but attending church gave him hope that he will be something, and he grew closer to God. He attributes this as the foundation of where he is today.

"That's why I put people first, because of God." – Luvuyo.

Luvuyo feels he has been called to the work he is doing, and it is his faith that enables him to meet the many challenges he experiences. He recalls how there was a time when BEE provided opportunities for tenders and everyone was looking for "quick bucks", but he stayed with what he felt God had given him.

"I put Jesus in everything I do." – Luvuyo.

Both Luvuyo and Ralph now have investing in common. Ralph says the first lesson he learnt is that investing is partnership, and that it doesn't matter how much equity you may own in the company - if the MD is the MD, it's their business. So it's very important to make sure the potential partner has the intelligence, integrity, energy and alignment of faith that builds trust. When it comes to serving on a board, he has learnt that the role is mostly cheerleading for the leaders, because running a business is really hard. Also, to remain patient and recognize the importance of 'Plan B' because initial business plans seldom work.

Most significantly, Ralph now finds himself asking when considering investment, *"Where is the golden thread of the gospel? Where is the golden thread of a redemption message?"* He cites Jesus' teaching in Matthew 25: 31-46 and its searching questions, *'When did I feed you, clothe you, or visit you in prison?'* When he speaks to businesses, he refers to Luvuyo's example and asks them, *"Where is your upside-down photocopier box? Where is your opportunity to serve other people?"* His question to himself is, *"How do I weave a redemption message into what I am doing and what I am backing?"*

In the South African context, where there were not many black businesses and very few role models when Luvuyo started his business, Luvuyo sees himself as a "first generation role model" with a responsibility to pass on the lessons he has learnt to enable others to create wealth and employment and deal with the systematic, structural challenges. He feels he has a responsibility to take what he and his partners have done and scale it, growing and supporting others and sharing the insights learnt, demonstrating to local entrepreneurs that it is possible for them to do the same thing. In addition, he is attempting to "mobilize the ecosystem" which includes not only investors, but also the universities so that there can be a growing understanding of the informal township sector through data gathering and case studies.

Luvuyo's focus is now on the wider horizon of the African continent. His hope is that God's blessing will come to the continent and that it will rise to influence the world positively through 'ubuntu' values which put people first in everything. Africa has its own solutions; it is now time for the sleeping giant to rise. He is inspired by the vibrancy, energy and hunger of the youthful population. His message to them is not to look to government but to entrepreneurship models on their own terms with their own solutions, not those of the West, for those solutions conflict with where young Africans find themselves.

Together, Luvuyo and Ralph model what it means to walk humbly, listen deeply and to put people first. They show that real impact comes through listening, humility, patient partnership and faith.

Key Themes and Insights

People Before Profit as the Foundation of Impact: The story of Silulo began not with a polished pitch, but with mutual trust. As Colin recounts, TBN's first investment in Silulo was driven not by numbers, but by a deep belief in Luvuyo as a person. Ralph noticed an upside-down photocopy box of handwritten CVs in the corner — a testament to Luvuyo's efforts in helping community members with job applications. This small, unglamorous service revealed the enterprise's genuine social heart. For Ralph, the handwritten CVs were further proof that this people-centred business, driven by Luvuyo's care for his community, held real potential for impact. Colin emphasizes how this simple yet bold act of belief became the foundation of something transformative.

"It's 50% about the people and 50% about the idea. But in truth, the first 50% is the people." – Ralph.

"There are many stories of Black entrepreneurs with amazing ideas, but without belief and seed capital, they can't grow." – Luvuyo.

Faith as Strategy, Anchor, and a Leadership Model: For all three, faith is not a private matter; it serves as a compass for leadership. Ralph reflects on Jesus as a model of leadership grounded in service, humility, and empowerment. Luvuyo shares how his faith was shaped by his mother's resilience, and by a year spent waiting in faith when he could not afford to attend university. Colin ties these perspectives together, highlighting their shared conviction that work is worship and entrepreneurship is a calling. For these men, faith is not abstract; it is practical, guiding decisions on hiring, mentoring, and investment, while shaping both the enterprise culture and the relational ecosystem that sustained Silulo's growth.

"I treat my work as a ministry ... I've been called to do this work, and at the centre is God." – Luvuyo.

"We all share a love for the Lord and that has shaped how we lead and how we invest." – Colin.

The Power of Belief and Seed Capital: When traditional systems excluded Luvuyo, who was blacklisted and unable to get bank loans, Ralph and others from the TBN network, including co-founder Dr Kim Tan, took a bold step of faith-driven investment. That £20,000 (R500,000) became more than capital: It was a symbol of trust; a belief in the person and his vision. Colin, who helped facilitate the transaction, remembers the joy and shock of betting on a team with no business plan and no formal credit backing. For Luvuyo, that moment symbolised a turning point, not just in business, but in being seen and believed in. It's a reminder of how critical both early-stage capital and affirmation are for entrepreneurs, especially in under-served contexts.

"That money was big money. It was the seed to what we have today. Without it, we might still be sitting in one café." – Luvuyo.

Servant Leadership and Succession: For all three men, leadership means uplifting others. Luvuyo designed Silulo to enable staff to transition into franchise owners and leaders in their own right. Today, Luvuyo mentors entrepreneurs through his foundation, stepping back from day-to-day operations. Ralph emphasizes that the best leaders focus on facilitating growth and succession rather than exerting control, ensuring the mission endures beyond the founder. Colin highlights how both have become role models, planting seeds in others and creating space for emerging leaders. Through structured mentorship, Silulo leaders learn to step back, empower others, and replicate the model in new townships, extending the company's impact far beyond a single location.

"Leadership means making yourself redundant." – Ralph.

"You've moved from leading a business to investing in others. You're multiplying yourselves." – Colin.

Fellowship Across Cultures and Home-based Hospitality: What began as a business relationship evolved into fellowship born through hospitality, mutual learning, and deep friendship. Colin's relational approach laid the foundation for enduring connections, inviting Luvuyo into his network and Ralph into his country, thereby building cross-cultural bridges that remain strong. Staying in Ralph's home and engaging with his family shaped how Luvuyo now raises his own children, so deeply impacted was he by shared meals and living under the same roof. This led to the transformation of professional trust into personal commitment, turning transactional interactions into transformational experiences. Luvuyo credits these moments with teaching him that true leadership is relational, not transactional, and that hospitality and cultural exchange can forge values and relationships that endure for decades.

"They didn't book me a hotel ... I stayed in Ralph's home. We ate together. That shaped how I raise my kids now." – Luvuyo.

"We wanted to build trust before we talked about capital." – Colin.

Vision, Adaptability, and Plan B: Business success, as all three agree, is rarely linear. Silulo started with a garage and an internet café. It grew by listening and responding to what people needed. Colin highlights how that early adaptability laid the groundwork for what became an integrated social franchise and support centre. All three emphasize the importance of vision, not as a rigid roadmap but as a compass. Luvuyo's humble beginning started with an internet café, from there adapting according to what people needed: Training, CV support, IT services and, later, entrepreneurship. Ralph stresses the necessity of being agile and thinking big – having 'Big Hairy Audacious Goals' - while always staying open to pivoting.

"The only thing I know about business plans is that they're wrong. The people that are truly successful in life are good at Plan B." – Ralph.

"We created a one-stop centre because the community showed us what they needed." – Luvuyo.

Resilience and Relationships to Overcome Systemic Barriers: Colin frames Luvuyo's rise from being previously blacklisted and operating out of a garage to leading one of South Africa's most impactful township businesses, as a powerful testament to resilience, hope and grace. Luvuyo's story not only reflects the structural inequalities many entrepreneurs face, but also illustrates how support, faith and grit can break through such barriers. Ralph shares how he instructed UK investors to enter investment relationships in foreign countries humbly, by listening to understand the local context, Together, Ralph and Luvuyo reveal how humility, relationship and truly listening can counter systemic barriers.

"We were blacklisted; no bank would touch us. But TBN believed in us." – Luvuyo.

"We don't understand this culture. Listen first!" – Ralph

"You're a true impact unicorn. But now it's about changing the whole ecosystem." – Colin.

Social Entrepreneurship as Legacy and Ecosystem Building: Silulo's impact has moved beyond profit to building an ecosystem by creating jobs, franchises and new businesses. Luvuyo is now a mentor to others, leading policy advocacy for social entrepreneurship, and driving a continental movement to support township and grassroots innovators. His work demonstrates that scaling impact requires going beyond personal success to replicate models, shift narratives and create enabling environments. Colin notes that what Luvuyo has achieved encapsulates the essential features of a first-generation ecosystem builder: To plant seeds for others and grow models that can scale, replicate, and decentralize power. He identifies this as a calling.

"The problem in Khayelitsha is the same as we'll see in Uganda, Nigeria ... the future is in the township." – Luvuyo.

Hope, Redemption, and the Future of Africa: In closing their conversation, Colin draws out their shared belief in the future, both spiritual and entrepreneurial. Ralph is focusing on integrating redemption into all his ventures, and Luvuyo is championing Africa's potential through advocacy and mentorship. Colin reminds listeners that hope is not naïve; it is the engine of innovation, inclusion and change. Their final message is this: Invest in people, stay rooted in faith, and believe in a better tomorrow.

"My hope is in the Lord ... My question now is, how do I weave a redemption message into what I'm doing?" – Ralph.

"It's the time for Africa to be able to rise now ... We have the solution among ourselves." – Luvuyo.

Key Principles for Faith-Driven Entrepreneurs

1. Lead with People, Not Profit

Build your business around people, not projections. Character, trust and relationships are more reliable predictors of success than spreadsheets or polished pitches. Colin emphasizes how belief in Luvuyo as a person, despite being blacklisted, was the reason TBN took the risk. Investing in individuals with integrity and heart will often yield long-term impact that outlasts profit margins.

"The first 50% is the people." – Ralph.

"Impact starts with relationship. Without trust, there's no traction." – Colin.

"Africa ... could show this world that we've got these deep values of who I am because of you. And these are values that put humanity at the centre, putting people first in everything." - Luvuyo.

2. Let Faith Guide the Mission

Faith serves as a source of strength, clarity, and resilience in leadership. For Colin, Ralph and Luvuyo, business is not just commerce but a form of ministry and a practice of servant leadership. Faith provides the courage to act boldly while grounding them in humility to serve others. It shapes not only their sense of purpose but also the very architecture of impact, influencing how teams are built, how capital is stewarded, and how justice and compassion are structurally embedded in business practice. Guided by faith, their values, decisions and purpose remained anchored. Every strategic choice, from franchise expansion to community engagement, is filtered through questions of service, stewardship and justice.

"Whenever I've been open with staff or clients, my position in faith has improved my standing in their eyes, not been detrimental to it. We as Christians in business are scared sometimes of talking about these things and talking about our beliefs. And I don't think we should be. As I say, it has never once been to my detriment." - Ralph

"I treat my work as a ministry... I've been called to do this work, and at the centre is God." – Luvuyo.
"We're called to walk out our faith practically ... in strategy, in service, in systems." – Colin.

3. Invest in People's Potential

Belief in people is often the true catalyst for transformation. The early investment in Silulo was not based on flawless business plans or bankable assets, but on character and calling. As Colin emphasizes, belief must come before scale. Real impact unfolds when people are trusted and empowered before they have "proven" themselves by conventional standards. Many of Silulo's earliest franchisees were former staff members who have since grown into successful branch owners and now mentor the next generation of entrepreneurs, extending the cycle of empowerment.

"The seed was not just money. It was belief." – Luvuyo.

"This wasn't just a loan. It was family." – Colin.

4. Adopt Servant Leadership

True leadership means making yourself less necessary over time, creating space for others to thrive. For Colin, Ralph and Luvuyo this principle is lived out through mentoring, succession, and platforming others. Luvuyo's joy in stepping back and Colin's passion for systems that decentralize power both embody the model of servant leadership. Lead by serving your team, sharing power and enabling others to succeed — even beyond your own role or organization.

5. Be Resilient and Keep Going

Entrepreneurship is rarely smooth. Luvuyo's journey from being blacklisted to building an award-winning enterprise shows the power of grit, faith and perseverance. Colin emphasizes that meaningful transformation often starts with rejection by systems not made for you — and that's where resilience becomes the differentiator. Don't let systemic barriers or slow starts stop you from believing in what's possible. Walk through barriers with faith, courage and collaboration.

"We were blacklisted but TBN believed in us." – Luvuyo.

"Running a business is hard. That's why we cheerlead, not criticize." – Ralph.

"Don't confuse slow progress with failure. Resilience builds real impact." – Colin.

6. Scale with Vision and Be Ready to Pivot

Have a bold, inspiring vision but don't be afraid to adapt and evolve. Stay responsive to what communities actually need. Colin describes Silulo as an example of community-led innovation – always grounded, always iterating. Be clear on your "why," flexible on your "how," and always remain open to discovering a better way.

"Vision should be rooted in people's needs, not just numbers." – Colin.

"We started with CVs and cafés. Now we're shaping

ecosystems." – Luvuyo.

7. Blend Profit with Purpose

Don't separate business from impact. By aligning financial and social outcomes, more resilient systems and accountable leadership are created. Social entrepreneurship isn't a compromise; it's a multiplier. Aligning commercial goals with social outcomes paves the way for growth and community transformation to go hand in hand as seen through the success of Silulo, proving that purpose fuels sustainability.

"Impact and income are not in conflict. They multiply when aligned." – Colin.

"Entrepreneurship is a solution for the continent … Once you are making money, you are making a difference in your community now … the kinds of things that make me selflessly say, 'I'm not perfect … but with what I've built, I can make some kind of a way to give to others.' And others can see and then they do it and be part of with this journey with me." – Luvuyo.

"When I'm speaking to businesses….I literally ask them… 'Where is your opportunity to serve other people?' I believe in blending social and commercial strategies. And I do believe that that's an advantage" - Ralph.

8. Be Generous with Presence, Not Just Capital

The most powerful investments are often relational rather than financial, grounded in presence, hospitality, and deep listening. Colin, Ralph and Luvuyo all emphasize that showing up matters far more than showing off. Shared meals, opened homes, and personal engagement create the fertile ground in which trust and transformation take root. Whether hosting a conversation, sharing a meal, or walking alongside a founder through challenges, these relational investments consistently generated far higher returns than capital alone.

"This journey wasn't just funded; it was shared." – Colin

9. Great Ventures Grow from Simple Acts of Service

Small acts of service like helping someone submit a job application or offering digital literacy training can have outsized ripple effects. One box of handwritten C.V.'s changed Ralph's view of Luvuyo's work. Colin encourages entrepreneurs and investors alike to be alert to the quiet signals of potential hidden in plain sight. Always be alert to simple, practical ways to serve others. That's where transformation begins.

"Impact often starts in the small, overlooked spaces." – Colin.

"Where is your upside-down photocopier box?" – Ralph.

Reflections in the Angello Network and the Acts Community Values

Whilst not explicitly named, the values of the early Acts church model - shared resources, community, radical generosity and living out faith practically - flow through this story. The collaboration between Luvuyo, Ralph and Colin reflects generosity, relational investment and shared purpose, moving far beyond transactional partnership. Ralph's hospitality, in welcoming Luvuyo into his home and family, represents the heart of Acts-style community which opens lives and resources to others. In turn, Luvuyo now practises this as he raises his own children and supports emerging entrepreneurs. The story illustrates the timeless power of integrating the values of radical generosity, shared resources and mentorship into modern entrepreneurship.

"You build deeper trust when you open your home, not just your wallet." – Colin.

"People don't get out of bed to drive profit. They get out of bed to make a difference." – Ralph.

The alignment of faith and business values — loving your neighbour, building inclusive systems and choosing impact over ego — is clearly evident in the work and worldview of the three men. Through this story we see how faith-driven entrepreneurs not only build companies, they cultivate communities and embed values that shape future generations. These are not only business partnerships; they are communities of calling. Ralph, Luvuyo and Colin demonstrate Angello's mission in action: Identifying, mentoring and investing in entrepreneurs who are Christ-centred, community-rooted and impact-driven. Their journey is a masterclass in faithful investing – not just in capital, but in lives.

The Angello network's commitment to fellowship, mentorship and long-term partnership is embodied in this story. The roles of the Ralph, Luvuyo and Colin as investors, entrepreneurs and friends, model Angello's value of relational capital, showing how servant leadership multiplies. Together, they show that real impact flows from faith-filled friendship, long-term accompaniment and shared vision, and how this can be replicated across other partnerships and regions.

Future Vision

"Africa must rise. We've got the solution among ourselves. We can model a new way of doing business with humanity at the centre." – Luvuyo.

"This is Africa's moment ... not just to catch up, but to lead in new ways." – Colin

All three men see the future anchored in faith, people, and the rising potential of Africa through the next generation of leaders. Luvuyo is now investing in social entrepreneurs across the continent, mentoring leaders in multiple African countries while driving policy efforts through Africa Forward and championing ecosystem change. His Foundation has already trained five cohorts of entrepreneurs and now runs independently of his day-to-day involvement, a testament to both sustainability and the strength of his leadership development. What began with Silulo has grown into a model that informs policy advocacy and ecosystem building at a continental scale.

Ralph continues to challenge himself and others with the deeper question, *"Where is the golden thread of redemption in your business?"* For him, gospel values are transformative, shaping ventures where financial return is inseparable from lasting human and societal benefit. In every investment, he seeks to embed this principle of redemption, ensuring that profit and purpose are held together in service of greater good. Together and individually Ralph, Luvuyo and Colin are shaping ecosystems, challenging businesses to embed redemption, and building bridges for purpose-led entrepreneurs that reach across the globe.

Closing Reflections

The conversation between Colin, Ralph and Luvuyo reminds us that business is more than profit; it is a platform for restoration, opportunity and human dignity. Their stories challenge all entrepreneurs in fellowship to lead with integrity, serve with humility, and to believe deeply in people. Their shared insights are a message of hope and a call to action.

My hope is in the Lord. Increasingly, I'm asking: 'Where is the redemption message in what I'm backing?'" – Ralph

"Entrepreneurship is the solution for the continent. That's how social entrepreneurship becomes so important." – Luvuyo

"We're not just telling stories. We're laying stepping stones for the next generation." – Colin.

Discernment with Reuben Coulter

Introduction

Reuben Coulter is the founder of Ignis Global, an impact investment advisory serving family offices and foundations. (*See Reuben's bio in Appendix One*).

Through Angello and his broader career, Reuben has worked to bridge the gap between capital and impact, focusing on creating ecosystems that empower entrepreneurs in emerging markets. His experiences at the World Economic Forum and his pursuit of an MBA further broadened his understanding of how business, policy, and investment intersect to drive long-term, sustainable transformation. He is committed to fostering networks, institutions, and financial models that support local entrepreneurs, ensuring that economic empowerment becomes a key driver of lasting social change.

Leadership and Impact

Reuben's working life has been a journey shaped by faith, discernment, perseverance and a commitment to systemic change. It has unfolded through what he describes as *"incredibly formative burning bush moments"* in which God redirected his path. The first was experienced when he was just 17, having convinced his parents to allow him to backpack across Zimbabwe and Mozambique and do volunteer work with missionaries they knew in those countries. Mozambique had just emerged from civil war, and Reuben was struck by the devastation he witnessed – families losing children to treatable diseases, and communities struggling in an economic environment akin to the Middle Ages in Europe. He observed that the missionaries, though spiritually passionate, were professionally ill-equipped, parachuting in Western solutions that quickly failed. Seeing expensive farm machinery not designed for local conditions rust by the roadside, Reuben realised that good intentions alone were not enough. In that moment, he made a promise to himself to make a difference, and to do it with excellence.

Reuben's conviction that he was called to make a difference led him to specialise in public health. He began working with Tearfund, which partners with churches in over 50 of the world's poorest countries to tackle poverty and injustice through sustainable development and responding to disasters. Reuben served with them in African crisis zones such as Darfur, Liberia, and Congo. The work was vital, but over time he recognised its limits; charitable aid was a temporary bandage on much deeper wounds. Without economic opportunities, people remained trapped in cycles of poverty and conflict. Reuben began to wonder whether business could be the engine for sustainable change.

Reuben's second *"burning bush moment"* occurred during a dinner conversation with a philanthropist about the work Tearfund was doing in Cambodia. Reuben shared with him stories of women rebuilding their lives after coming out of trafficking and sex work, and it happened that the philanthropist's business worked with factories in Cambodia. Reuben realised that he could assist him to use his business as a "force for good" by applying his philanthropic capital to micro-businesses and livelihood projects under the umbrella of Tearfund; in that way, they would be complementing each other and could create something impactful and sustainable.

Initially, Reuben thought he had stumbled upon this insight alone, but he soon discovered the Transformational Business Network, where leaders like Dr. Kim Tan, founder of TBN, and Malcolm Johnston, founder of Angello, were already championing this vision of business as a force for good. Reuben realized he needed to have a much deeper appreciation of how business works and how it can succeed in developing economies, if he was to be of real support in this sector. Collaboration within these networks led to an opportunity to lead the Africa portfolio for the World Economic Forum and to study towards an MBA at the same time. In this way, he developed a deeper understanding of parliaments and boardrooms while learning about business and gaining practical business skills.

Reuben's work now centres on bridging entrepreneurs with the capital resources they need as well as mentorship, skills-development and enabling ecosystems. He advocates for impact investment models that are both ethical and effective, ensuring that businesses in emerging markets are equipped to thrive. Reuben's concept of impact has been influenced by Andy Crouch, who is a partner for theology and culture at Praxis, an organization that works as a creative engine for redemptive entrepreneurship. Reuben describes Andy's insight that the definition of impact is an object coming into forcible contact with another – a blow, and most of us recoil from a blow… the momentum is not sustained. So, while the impact might look flashy with high potential, it doesn't necessarily lead to lasting transformation. Because the net force on an object is equal to the change in its momentum divided by the time over which the change occurs, Reuben has discerned that the challenge is to seek after sustained influence by establishing lasting relationships - people coming together with a common purpose and encouraging, supporting and equipping one another. He explains that Influence is relationship multiplied by time, and it's about a dense network of people coming together.

Reuben has learnt that relational impact can feel slow and sometimes even painful, but over a long enough period it can bear a huge amount of fruit. He feels that this is an accurate description of the Angello network and the friendships they have been able to form over the years.

Challenges and Lessons

The hard truth Reuben learnt from his work at the World Economic Forum is that at the macroeconomic policy level the focus is more about changing the optics and improving the narrative than delivering real, substantive change. As someone who cares deeply about making a difference on the ground and really delivering impact, not just talking about it, he became frustrated with the World Economic Forum and began to turn his attention to what he could do to provide tangible support for entrepreneurs in emerging economies to help them succeed.

Entrepreneurs were approaching him in the hope that he could connect them with people with investment capital, but Reuben realised they needed much more – they needed an ecosystem that would help them flourish. An enabling environment has a pool of skilled employees, access to a thriving economic market with potential customers, a banking system to lend initial capital and a favourable tax policy. He began to think about how to build a system that would enable these entrepreneurs to succeed, because providing capital alone is not enough. He decided to make contact again with Dr Kim Tan and the TBN, because they were thinking in similar ways and were motivated by faith, and he could bring his skills and expertise to bear in what they were doing.

One of the key challenges Reuben identifies in pursing long-term transformation is the difficulty of moving beyond movements to building institutions that can sustain long-term impact. While movements can inspire change through igniting passion and sparking momentum, without structures to carry a vision forward, they risk fading as quickly as they rise. Sound educational, financial and organisational institutions provide the necessary structure and stability to ensure transformation endures across generations.

He also underscores the importance of local leadership alongside the development of supporting organisations and investment funds to nurture entrepreneurship in emerging markets. Transformation cannot be imposed from the outside. It requires ecosystems rooted in context, with local supporting organisations and investors nurturing entrepreneurship from within.

Another significant challenge lies in changing investor mindsets, particularly in shifting perceptions of how capital should be deployed to drive both social and financial returns. Too often, capital is divided into "doing good" through philanthropy and "making returns" through business. Reuben challenges this mindset, arguing that sustainable change requires integrating both. Building relational partnerships which foster trust between investors and local entrepreneurs is key to creating a thriving and sustainable economic environment that delivers both social and financial outcomes.

Reuben cites the importance of **people, patience, persuasion, and platforms** when overcoming challenges:

"You don't do it alone so find others who you can build deep, trusted relationships with."

Reuben's advice is that having identified the **people** you think you can journey with, it's important to test those relationships. There may be a common vision, but approaches may very different. Just because someone shares that common vision or shares a common faith does not necessarily mean that they're going to be the person you want to go on a journey with. He emphasises the importance of making sure you have the same underpinning values.

"That's the only thing that will sustain you over the long run."

Further, being the initial visionary does not mean that your vision is obvious to everybody else. To deliver long-term change requires **patience** and persuasion.

"The danger with prophets and pioneers is we rush ahead and we're too impatient to bring other people with us, and we need to be really careful with that, otherwise we'll be gone within a generation, and we won't have left a legacy of kind of lasting change."

For change to be lasting, there must be the appropriate institutions – **platforms** that will appropriately sustain the long-term trajectory. By way of example, Reuben refers to the first industrial revolution and universities such as Princeton and Yale, and many others which were founded as seminaries by people of faith to equip and train the next generation.

"We just aren't seeing those grow and develop. And so I think we need to be very thoughtful. 'Okay, what are the institutions which are going to help this movement endure for 100, 200, 1000 years? How do we build for the long term?'"

Key Themes and Insights

Discernment, Direction and Purpose: Reuben Coulter speaks of "burning bush moments" as divine prompts that recalibrate one's direction toward meaningful, purpose-driven work. These revelations represent a pattern of spiritual discernment in which God called him to realign his path with deeper purpose. Recognising and responding to these moments means aligning personal conviction with professional calling. Reuben's experience of these moments invites others to consider how spiritual insight and lived experience can inspire creative approaches to impact, serving as a reminder that leadership rooted in faith requires attentiveness to God and a willingness to act to influence and transform inadequate systems.

"Life is composed of what I call 'burning bush' moments ... God grabs our attention and directs it in a new way."

"Children were dying, and I was just really convicted by God that actually I needed to do something about this. I needed to be part of the solution...17-year-old me promised that I wanted to make a difference, and I wanted to do it with excellence."

Business as a Force for Good: Redefining the Engine of Development: Reuben challenges the traditional divide between charity and enterprise by positioning ethical business designed with integrity as a more sustainable pathway to social change. His insight reframes business from a profit-making enterprise to a morally grounded platform for empowerment. In his view, when businesses are designed and led with integrity, they become scalable solutions to poverty and inequality. Reuben's involvement in global networks has been shaped by the conviction that well-structured enterprises can build dignity, agency and resilience in communities often left behind by donor-driven aid models.

"I realised that his business could do far more good than my charity could do."

Faith-Driven Entrepreneurship: Integrating Conviction and Commerce: Reuben advocates integrating faith into business, ensuring that social and spiritual values are embedded within business models rather than treated as external considerations. He sees this mindset reflected in organisations like B Corps and faith-driven business networks which emphasise ethical leadership, responsible capitalism and purpose-driven operations.

"We're seeing entrepreneurs realize, 'Actually, I can build a business and do good at the same time, and how I treat my employees and my customers and the community doesn't need to be an afterthought, but actually can have powerful, beneficial effects for my bottom line as well. I can build that into my business model.'"

The Power of Relationships and Networks: Trust as Infrastructure: Reuben sees networks not just as professional tools but as relational ecosystems that cultivate trust, accountability and long-term collaboration. Drawing from the cultural examples of Somali and Ismaili communities, he emphasises the strategic value of interdependence — how businesses rooted in mutual trust weather adversity better and scale more organically. For faith-based entrepreneurs, the message is clear: Surround yourself with a community that reinforces your values and multiplies your impact.

"The power of relationships is incredible. And the great thing is, it compounds over time."

Perseverance and the Role of Community: Endurance in the Quiet Work: Reuben reminds us that transformation doesn't come quickly — and often, not visibly. He lifts the curtain on the often-unseen persistence behind mission-driven work. More than grit, it's the presence of a faith-aligned community that enables people to stay the course. In a culture obsessed with speed and scale, Reuben's lesson is countercultural: Lasting change requires time, patience, and companions on the journey.

"Perseverance ... it just takes time. There's no shortcuts to it, and it's not glamorous, it's not flashy."

"Having other people who have a similar mindset, a heart, and are able to encourage you through the ups and downs, that journey is just incredibly valuable."

Building Institutions, Not Just Movements: Structuring for Sustainability: Reuben urges visionaries not to stop at inspiration. While movements energise and mobilise, institutions are what anchor and sustain progress. He advocates for building structures — educational, financial, and organisational — that can carry the weight of vision across generations. The insight here is strategic: Passion initiates change, but only intentional design ensures its longevity.

"Movements burn bright, but they can burn out. What movements need behind them are institutions that preserve direction and capability over the long term."

Mobilising Capital for Greater Impact: Aligning Resources with Purpose: For Reuben, faith-driven impact must be backed by intentional capital. He challenges the disconnect between mission and money, calling for a reallocation of financial resources that reflect kingdom values. It's not enough to have good intentions; those intentions must be resourced. He envisions a future where investment portfolios and philanthropic strategies are fully integrated with the call to serve and uplift others through business and innovation.

"We need to get that 90% (of capita) into the game and fully aligned with the purposes that we're called for."

Key Principles for Faith-Driven Entrepreneurs

1. Be Open to Divine Inspiration

Stay attuned to the pivotal moment that Reuben calls "burning bush moments," where God may redirect your path toward greater impact. These moments of clarity can shape your purpose and guide you toward meaningful, faith-driven work.

2. Leverage Business as a Force for Good

Recognise that business can be a powerful tool for sustainable social change. Move beyond charity by embedding ethical principles into your operations, ensuring that your business actively contributes to economic empowerment and long-term development.

3. Build Deep, Trusted Relationships

Success in faith-driven entrepreneurship is not a solo journey. Surround yourself with a strong network of like-minded individuals who share your values and vision. These relationships provide encouragement, resources, and accountability, strengthening your impact over time.

4. Embrace a Long-Term Perspective

Systems change and sustainable transformation takes time. Perseverance is key - there are no shortcuts. Stay committed to your mission, even when progress seems slow, and rely on a supportive community to navigate challenges.

5. Integrate Faith into Business

Ensure that your faith-driven values are not just an afterthought but are embedded in your business model. How you treat employees, customers and stakeholders should reflect your spiritual and ethical principles.

6. Think Beyond Charity

While philanthropy has its place, sustainable impact often comes through economic empowerment. Shift from short-term relief efforts to long-term strategies that enable individuals and communities to thrive through entrepreneurship and business innovation.

7. Build Institutions, Not Just Movements

Movements can spark change, but institutions sustain it. Focus on creating financial, educational and business institutions that will endure for generations and provide long-term solutions to societal challenges.

Reflections on the Angello Network and the Acts Communtiy Values

Reuben identifies perseverance as the most helpful of the Acts Community values. He emphasises that influencing long-term systems change takes time

"There are no shortcuts to it; it's not glamorous, it's not flashy, it's just a long investment, and having other people who have a similar mindset and heart and are able to encourage you through the ups and downs, that journey is just incredibly valuable, because otherwise we just get discouraged and we go and do something else which is easier."

He appreciates that the Angello network enables faith-driven entrepreneurs to speak into each other's lives and to sharpen and refine each other's thinking. He points out that there are not many people who understand systems thinking and the role it can play, so having a group in which systems thinking is fundamental to its approach is truly valuable. Furthermore, although they do not gather as often as they would like, the members are scattered widely and act as salt to many other networks. Because many in the Angello network have been on this journey for quite a long time, they bring wisdom and experience.

"Hopefully we can bring experience and a little bit of wisdom to some of the newer entrants who are coming with big hearts but can kind of rush into a situation and either have no impact or often cause more harm than good."

Reuben sees Angello's vision of bridging the gap between the rich and the poor through business as essential to creating sustainable economic transformation. He shares examples of successful initiatives such as the Wellers Impact Fund, which helps non-profits leverage their property assets to generate sustainable income, reducing reliance on external funding.

Reuben's experience of systems in the African context has provided him with significant insights into operations that disrupt Westernised Christian thinking. He points out that describing the Angello network as an Acts Community is *"a deeply challenging aspiration."*

"Most of us kind of gloss over the bits in Acts which are a little bit uncomfortable, or, as our American friends would like to call it, are quite Marxist in their nature, which is 'They had all things in common' and how they stewarded their finances for the common good. I think that's an incredible but a deeply challenging aspiration for any of us."

Reuben describes how the Ismaili and Somali communities are two of the most successful business groups in East Africa. The Ismaili are a Muslim minority group, and the Somalis are refugee immigrants in Kenya from Somalia who run the vast majority of shops. Many Kenyans are deeply suspicious of how they have become come so successful. Reuben explains that their "secret" is the deep, trusted relationships that the community has with one another.

"In the case of the Somali community, if you arrive in a new town and you're a Somali, you're vetted and invited to join their kind of Community Savings and Loan Bank, and they ask you to put capital into this group. So you might put $10,000 into the savings and when you come to start your business, they will lend you that money as an uncollateralized loan and provide you with the networks and support to enable your business to get started, and they'll really back you and enable you to succeed."

The Ismaili community is similar, but they do it in a more structured way. They have a number of core anchor businesses in particular towns and cities owned by their community foundation; the profits from these businesses then go into hospitals and universities which are some of the best in Africa, and that wins them political favour.

By comparison, most Christian communities are individualistic. Reuben points out the need to be much more intentional about developing trust, and to be sacrificial in supporting and enabling each other to succeed. His hope is that the Acts Community can move to another level and find structured ways to do so, with models that can be replicated to support the common good. He stresses the need for trusted communities and networks within the Christian business community, recognising that deep relationships and shared values can significantly enhance success.

Reuben is deeply committed to advancing Angello's vision internationally by fostering sustainable business ecosystems and empowering entrepreneurs in emerging economies. He recognises that long-term economic transformation requires more than just financial investment: It necessitates a comprehensive approach that includes skills development, market access and supportive infrastructure. He emphasises the significance of perseverance, recognising that long-term systems change requires patience, resilience and sustained effort. He believes that transformation does not happen overnight but is the result of years of commitment and steady progress. Reuben also values the power of relationships, highlighting how trust and collaboration compound over time to create lasting impact.

Reuben highlights the significance of creating an enabling environment where businesses can thrive. He acknowledges that entrepreneurship does not happen in isolation; rather, it flourishes within strong networks of trust and collaboration. Through Angello, he works to cultivate relationships that provide ongoing support, ensuring that business leaders not only gain access to opportunities but also have the resilience and guidance needed to create lasting impact. He emphasises the importance of collaboration, long-term systems thinking, and the power of relationships and networks such as the Angello network and the Transformational Business Network in fostering enduring change.

Future Vision

Reuben identifies the core paradigm of the Angello network as empowering and equipping local leaders by coming alongside and behind them, rather than stepping in and bringing leadership from the outside. He identifies Luvuyo Rani as an example of the fruit that is to come in future decades. Luvuyo has now featured at several World Economic Forum conferences, has set up his own Foundation, and is encouraging and equipping many other entrepreneurs. All this from a few people coming around him and praying with him.

Reuben is upbeat about the future. He regards this season of building movements as *"incredibly exciting, because you're casting a new vision, a new paradigm of how transformation* happens in the world and in church circles and development circles. For many, many decades the prime movers were non-profits or churches ... they were the ones expected to bring spiritual, social and environmental transformation. But the reality was that there were limitations to their ability to deliver, and the business leader and the investor was very much seen as the person who writes the cheques for the people who do good. I think there's now a realization that that is not a sustainable model, and it completely undervalues the skills of the entrepreneur and investor. Actually, by embedding social purpose and spiritual purpose into their operating models, entrepreneurs and investors can achieve sustainable, scalable good."

Reuben sees himself as an institution builder, a bridge-maker between those who have capital and those who need capital, ensuring that it's redeployed in the most effective way all around the world – a difficult but "incredibly exciting" challenge. Looking ahead, Reuben hopes to build institutions that serve as conduits for capital and connections, ensuring that resources flow effectively to where they are most needed. He envisions a future where entrepreneurs are supported by a mature ecosystem of local leadership and business support networks that will provide them with the mentorship, funding, and opportunities required for success. Additionally, he aims to connect pioneering investors with second movers, recognising that many investors may not have direct experience in emerging markets but can benefit from partnerships with those who do. By facilitating these connections, he seeks to ensure that capital is deployed wisely and effectively for "good."

Closing Reflections

The consistent metaphor applied by Reuben throughout this compelling conversation is that of a bridge.

"Imagine a bridge ... with any bridge, it's completely unstable until it's completed. And so a 60% bridge, or an 80% bridge, *is a highly dangerous thing ... it's made up of many different parts and components. So we just get overwhelmed to kind of go, oh my goodness, where do we start in building bridges?"*

Reuben's answer to the question of where to start is to lay good foundations. He is encouraged that in certain cities and countries, an ecosystem of local entrepreneurial leadership is beginning to mature. This is essential if capital if is to be invested effectively.

"If you deploy capital into a place which is not ready for it, it's a bit like torrential rain falling on hard ground; it'll hit the hard ground and it'll wash away all your topsoil and probably do more harm than good. The ground has to be prepared ... it has to be furrowed, and that really needs local leaders with a common vision for country and place. We're beginning to see that. I can look at countries like Romania, like Pakistan, like Egypt, and we're just beginning to see that come together at a local level."

The second component needed for the bridge are the supporting pillars - organizations which come alongside to disciple and equip and invest in businesses. These must be developed locally and Reuben has observed that they are beginning to form.

"We're beginning to see business support networks, incubators, accelerators, develop and mature in these different countries, and we're slowly but surely beginning to see investment funds emerge which are targeted towards these specific types of businesses, and those investment funds are beginning to develop capacity to do this at scale."

Reuben cautions that much education is required when it comes to investors. He describes a chasmic divide between the extremes of philanthropy, where money is given away, and investing where the sole goal is to maximize financial returns. He reflects that the challenge is to persuade investors to adopt a new paradigm by blending the two. The traditional investing tools of venture capital or private equity may not be suitable in emerging markets.

"Successful investors often want to kind of come in and take what they have done in their home market and deploy it into a new market, and that rarely succeeds."

The third phase of building the bridge is to link the supporting pillars. This is done by building relational partnerships with mutual trust and confidence between international investors and local investing partners and, in turn, between them and the local entrepreneurs. For this, other types of financial instruments and measures of expectation may be required.

Reuben emphasises the importance of learning from diverse perspectives and building bridges between Christian and secular counterparts to enhance mutual understanding and cooperation. He encourages investing time in learning and equipping each other, believing that long-term success comes from shared wisdom and continuous growth. By fostering deeper collaboration and strengthening institutional foundations, he remains committed to advancing Angello's mission and supporting the next generation of Kingdom-minded entrepreneurs.

Service with Duncan Parker and Kehkshan Newton

Introduction

In this conversation **Kehkshan Newton** of Pak Mission Society and **Duncan Parker,** a faith-driven impact investor and leader, share their transformative journeys with the Angello Network. Committed to humanitarian development, entrepreneurial innovation and Christ-centred values, both leaders reflect on how their personal callings and professional paths have converged around a shared conviction that enterprise-led development grounded in Godly principles can bring lasting, systemic change to communities in need. Their stories offer inspiration and practical insight for entrepreneurs navigating the intersection of faith, business and purpose, highlighting the power of ecosystems, leadership and spiritual resilience in shaping a better world. (*See bios of Kehkshan and Duncan in Appendix One*).

Pak Mission Society (PMS) strives to fulfil the Great Commission within a Muslim majority context, engaging in holistic community development programmes with a Christian worldview. Kehkshan Newton leads the youth leadership and economic empowerment portfolio at PMS. She has a degree in engineering and Masters' qualifications in international development and social sciences. Her research field is entrepreneurial ecosystems, specifically Christian entrepreneurial ecosystems in Pakistan, and the barriers encountered by Christian women trying to enter the world of business in that country. Kehkshan left a job with one of the leading telecom companies in Pakistan to provide assistance to rural women - and soon began to consider the empowering potential of entrepreneurship for unskilled, illiterate women. Meeting Malcolm Johnston of the Angello Development Foundation (ADF) inspired her to explore enterprise-led development, applying Acts Community values. Facilitating entrepreneurship has become her calling — a way to live her faith with purpose and bring solutions that create dignity, opportunity, and lasting change.

Duncan Parker is a Group Chief Executive for a private family concern which creates and nurtures entrepreneurial businesses that can then invest in other purpose-led enterprises and impactful organizations. Duncan's early career was in international development. His initial thinking was that microfinance "was the answer to the world's problems" until he came to realise that purpose-led enterprise and job-creation has an even further reach in "doing good for people and planet." He has been involved with the Angello network for over 15 years, having met Malcolm Johnston at a launch for an ethical investment fund to invest in agriculture across Sub-Saharan Africa.

Leadership and Impact

Kehkshan Newton's motivation to join the Angello network was born out of a lifelong awareness of struggle and injustice. From the age of twelve, she carried a conviction that poverty was the root cause of multiple societal ills and hardships. Growing up in a country she describes as a "supermarket of disasters" marked by economic fragility and social vulnerability, she saw how poverty affected lives painfully and destructively. Within marginalized Christian communities in Pakistan the challenges were even greater, and for women the situation was harsher still.

Kehkshan's conviction that she was "born for a purpose" has shaped her leadership at Pak Mission Society. The vision of PMS is to enable fullness of life, and for the first 15 years of its existence its focus was on humanitarian assistance. When Kehkshan joined the organization in 2019 a strategic review had revealed the need to move beyond humanitarian assistance, and they began thinking about business as the vehicle to transform communities and create a generation of Christian leaders. Kehkshan explains that interaction with Angello and other faith-driven business networks has transformed the thinking pattern of the organization. Since 2020, Kehkshan has helped lead PMS through a remarkable transformation from a traditional humanitarian aid organization to a dynamic, hybrid model of social enterprises dedicated to uplifting vulnerable and disaster-stricken communities. The organization now nurtures over 10,000 entrepreneurs in their own network across Pakistan. Defined by vision, courage and a deep-rooted commitment to empowering marginalized Christian women and youth, Kehkshan's work exemplifies her belief that faith and enterprise together can create generational change.

"We had a dream ... to have a generation of Christian leaders who can lead the marketplace in Pakistan ... a generation of Christian leaders who can talk to the global north to recalibrate their thinking patterns." – Kehkshan.

Duncan Parker's journey has been shaped by a similar search for sustainable solutions to poverty. Years of work in humanitarian aid showed him that aid and the provision of finance to low-income groups without access to banking services could address urgent needs, but they treated the symptoms rather than the root causes of poverty. Duncan became convinced that the real drivers of economic transformation are enterprises that create jobs and enable people to take charge of their own future.

This conviction re-shaped the second half of his career, leading him into entrepreneurship, impact investment and business-building. Duncan starts and supports businesses, creates investment funds, and works to direct capital into solutions that serve both people and planet. His leadership is grounded in humility, radical encouragement and an unwavering commitment to stewardship and impact. Inspired by the early Christian leader Barnabas 'the Encourager,' Duncan seeks to combine faith with practical action, mobilizing wealth and resources as a force for lasting change.

Kehkshan and Duncan embody leadership styles that blend faith, strategy, stewardship and service. Both have embraced enterprise as a vehicle for sustaining dignity, hope and transformation. Their work reflects a shared conviction that faith-driven entrepreneurship, supported by community and grounded in Kingdom values, has the power to address poverty at its roots and shape a more just and hopeful future.

Challenges and Lessons

Kehkshan credits conferences like Forge and the interaction with Angello and other faith-driven business networks with influencing Pak Mission Society to explore its own potential as a convening power able to gather stakeholders, rivals, and other relevant bodies to foster collective action, create solutions and drive progress. This has been a mind-shift within the organization, which now accepts that capital is not the only thing required for building businesses - they also require culture, connection and capacity building. Shifting this entrenched mindset has been slow and difficult, but vital to enable inclusive and sustainable models of enterprise-led development.

"Ecosystem mapping, along with the Angello network, really helped us to shift our mindset ... and the organization has taken a major shift in the last five years, moving from charity-led development to enterprise-led development." - Kehkshan

Both Kekshan and Duncan acknowledge the emotional and spiritual weight that comes with leading in challenging contexts. For Kehkshan, working in a volatile environment as a Christian woman leader has at times felt lonely and overwhelming. The global Angello community has provided essential encouragement and connection, reminding her and her colleagues that they are not alone in their mission.

"Sometimes you thought that you are alone in this whole journey ... it gave us a lot of encouragement that we are not alone." – Kehkshan.

Coming from an engineering background, Kehkshan initially sought clear, predictable paths in her work. One of her greatest lessons has been learning to trust God's incremental guidance rather than relying on fixed outcomes or defined destinations.

This lesson in spiritual surrender is echoed by Duncan's reflections on the limitations of resources and the importance of wise stewardship. He observes that although 'trade, not aid' has been a slogan in the UK since the turn of the century, together with the growing realisation that localization is the key, the global north may be part of the problem, not part of the solution. He has been conscious that providing financial resources from the north should not be a gift; it should be a sharing of resources, and the challenge is how to share the resources wisely. When he was working for a charitable NGO he knew he would never have enough resources to solve the problem and felt really sad that he could not provide all that was needed.

"I would never have enough resources to solve the problem… all I could do is give some catalytic capital to stimulate opportunities for change on the ground." – Duncan.

Duncan saw microfinance as a solution because the return of loans provided to start-ups enabled others to start. He then began to think about building businesses that would have a focused purpose to grow entrepreneurialism. He recalls having his thinking crystallized by an Angello colleague who pointed out that the entire pot of global philanthropy amounts to just 10% of what would be needed to achieve the Sustainable Development Goals; however, if less than 1% of global investable financial assets was moved into businesses that are purpose-led to impact the global issues covered by the SDGs, it would go a long way towards addressing the problems faced by 'people and planet.'

"Rather than grow the 10% of generosity that is needed, why don't you just divert less than 1% of global assets into doing good, rather than into just making money?" – Duncan.

This insight led Duncan into the "second part of his career" - convincing people with wealth to invest in purpose-led businesses. He is inspired by Kehkshan and subscribes to her conviction that ecosystems must be created if businesses are to survive. Such ecosystems have funders, incubators, accelerators, fellow-entrepreneurs, markets, and places where potential entrepreneurs are educated, trained and schooled. Duncan believes all this is possible to achieve, and he senses an increasing momentum towards consumers and investors wanting their money to do good and improve the planet.

Kehkshan admits to times when she and her colleagues feel low, especially when discouraged by their own people. However, they find inspiration through the Angello network's stories from other countries such as Romania, Mongolia, and Moldova. Knowing they are not alone on this journey gives them great encouragement. She and many others in her national network believe God is really working in Pakistan, and that they are being salt but not yet the light. Christians are only 2% of the population, but Kehkshan believes the light will be seen when the poverty-stricken and the illiterate are given a voice. To give women and the youth a voice is the inspiration behind the PMS programmes.

"The day will come when we will not only be the salt ... we will be the light of Pakistan as the market-based leaders of Pakistan." – Kehkshan.

Kehkshan testifies to a life-changing visit to Uganda through an Angello network initiative. To see the urban slums, and to witness how people were living there yet still determined in their faith and boldly proclaiming it, was extremely powerful and transforming. She acknowledges their own strength of having 10,000 entrepreneurs, but the challenge is how to support them, and how each can help the other to grow. She knows it will be a long journey, but she and her team believe in the power of miracles. They are determined to create impact in Pakistan.

The mental, emotional, spiritual, and systemic challenges Kehkshan and Duncan confront reveal the depth of faith and resilience required in purpose-driven leadership. However, they also provide encouraging lessons about the importance of transformation, trust, stewardship and the strength of community.

Key Themes and Insights

Enterprise-Led Development as a Solution to Poverty: Both Kehkshan and Duncan emphasize that while charitable aid plays a role, long-term and systemic change comes through enterprise. Kehkshan originally trained as an engineer but transitioned to grassroots entrepreneurship in response to the poverty she saw in her community. Her conviction grew through helping to lead Pak Mission Society's transformation from humanitarian aid to business-based solutions.

"If you are not literate, if you are not skilled, even then the power of entrepreneurship can change your life." – Kehkshan.

Duncan echoes this view, stating that employment and business are the most effective tools to break the cycle of poverty, noting from his development work that aid alone could never meet the scale of global needs.

Mindset Shift: From Charity Dependency to Entrepreneurial Empowerment: Kehkshan shares how the Angello network helped catalyse a transformation in thinking within her organization and community. Moving away from the belief that capital alone solves problems, they began focusing on building an entrepreneurial ecosystem based on culture, capacity, connection and capital. This shift in mindset fuelled the growth of a national network of 10,000 entrepreneurs across various business stages.

"Related to entrepreneurship, we require capital, we require culture, we require connection, we require capacity building." – Kehkshan.

Faith as the Anchor and Catalyst for Action: For both leaders, faith is not a separate compartment of life but the core driver of vision, action and resilience. Duncan describes faith as foundational to hope and essential to navigating a broken world.

"Without hope, we have nothing. The definition of faith is hope ... and it's love." – Duncan.

Kehkshan adds that she believed from an early age she was *"born for a purpose"* and sees entrepreneurship as a divine means to bring light into dark places.

Community, Fellowship, and the Acts Model: The Angello network's emphasis on the Acts Community model based on early Christian fellowship has been a powerful source of support and inspiration for both leaders. Kehkshan describes her experience of the Community as *"fresh air,"* especially in the volatile and marginalized context of Christian life in Pakistan.

The Power of Ecosystems: Both leaders emphasize the importance of surrounding entrepreneurs with ecosystems of support — mentors, investors, collaborators and educators. Duncan speaks about redirecting global resources toward impact by building strong, interdependent networks:

"Rather than grow the 10% of generosity that is needed, why don't you just divert less than 1% of global assets into doing good?" – Duncan.

This practical, scalable vision of change reinforces the importance of infrastructure and relationships in nurturing businesses with purpose.

Global Inspiration and Local Transformation: Hearing stories from entrepreneurs around the world, especially within the Angello network, provides vital encouragement. For Kehkshan, visiting Uganda through the Angello Young Tribe initiative deeply impacted her perspective on faith, poverty and leadership.

Key Principles For Faith-Driven Entrepreneurs

1. Trust in God's Timing and Process

Faith-driven entrepreneurs must learn to walk by faith, not sight. Kehkshan reminds us that God rarely reveals the entire path at once. God guides step by step, which requires patience, surrender and trust in His divine timing.

"Patience is required, and blind trust in God is required, that the Lord is leading your way." – Kehkshan.

2. Lead with Purpose, Not Position

True leadership is rooted in calling, not titles. Both Duncan and Kehkshan stress the importance of aligning one's work with God's greater purpose and moving beyond personal ambition to live a life of service.

"I am born for a purpose." – Kehkshan.

3. Build and Belong to Collaborative Ecosystems, not Silos

Entrepreneurs thrive in community. Surrounding oneself with capital, mentors, collaborators and encouragers is essential. Duncan and Kehkshan both emphasize the need to cultivate ecosystems that support growth and sustainability.

"I think that ecosystem mapping, along with the Angello network, really helps us to shift our own mindset." – Kehkshan.

4. Champion Enterprise-Led Development

Enterprise is not only a business model; it's also a vehicle for dignity, empowerment and long-term change. Duncan emphasizes that creating jobs allows people to take control of their own destiny.

"But the thing that really moves the dial, if you can try and get rid of poverty … is enterprise. It's creating jobs for people so that they can earn money and be in charge of their own destiny." – Duncan.

5. Hold Fast to Hope and Vision

Faith-driven entrepreneurship requires hope … a belief that change is possible. Vision, when shared with a supportive community, becomes a sustaining force despite the challenges.

6. Invest in the Next Generation

Legacy-minded leadership means creating space for others to rise. Kehkshan calls leaders to embrace succession, mentorship and elevation of young talent.

"It's very important to think of your next level, because your next level will give the space to the young ones who are coming behind you. So thinking of giving the space to the other one, and taking your next level, is very important to really give momentum to the country. You are not the sole owner of everything around you." – Kehkshan.

The above principles offer faith-driven entrepreneurs a practical, purpose-centred roadmap rooted in patience, purpose, ecosystem thinking and the courage to invest in others as God leads.

Reflections on the Angello Network and the Acts Community Values

Duncan relates that he may be responsible for suggesting that Angello is an Acts Community. He tells of a conversation with Angello colleagues in which he expressed his admiration for Barnabas, whose name means 'son of encouragement,' for influencing the disciples to share whatever they had amongst the believers in Judea during a severe famine (see Acts Ch. 11), suggesting that this may have been the first time the followers of Jesus committed to living the radical life Jesus taught about. Duncan promotes the idea that the book of Acts isn't finished:

"I think it's on Chapter a billion and something, you know, because 2025 years later we're still writing it; Kehkshan is writing it every day in her life." – Duncan.

Duncan concurs with Kehkshan that modern-day miracles are happening daily in the work people are doing for others, and advocates that they should be written down, as were the miracles in the Gospels and Book of Acts. He reminds us that there are many stories in which God can be seen at work, and that people are "still trying to be Christ, trying to do those things that Jesus said are beautiful and righteous." The values at work in the Angello network are the values of the original Acts Community: Generosity, fellowship, and service. Duncan declares that this is what Angello is about - trying to do these things individually and corporately and recognizing them when other people are doing them.

"We're still trying to be that community of people that live life counter-culturally to how the world would have us live." – Duncan.

Duncan reflects that this view of the community isn't idealized; it's grounded in real commitment. For him, the Angello network is a fellowship bound by vision and action, marked by shared resources, encouragement and faithful service across nations and cultures.

Kehkshan, navigating the volatility and complexity of life as a Christian leader in Pakistan, sees the Acts Community as a source of deep inspiration and strength, a striking contrast to the isolation and discouragement often faced in her context. For her, the Acts Community is not just an ideal but a lived reality — proof that faith, generosity and collaboration can thrive even in today's fragmented world.

She reflects that wherever a situation is volatile and uncertain or complex and ambiguous, she thinks about the community. In the book of Acts. When she first attended a session related to the values of the Acts Community it was "fresh air" for her, because in the context of Pakistan, where she and her colleagues are living as Christians, that enthusiasm and that excitement is missing. The concept of a community moving and spreading across the whole world, taking the message of God to the whole world despite the challenges, always moving forward in faith with excitement and enthusiasm, believing steadfastly in the road map given to them by God and all moving together on it, is very inspiring for her.

Kehkshan confesses that it is challenging in these times to be an Acts Community. The concept is easy to say, but difficult to practise in an individualistic world where everybody is focused on their own life, their own businesses, their own targets. However, she is energised by the Angello network's commitment to getting connected and supporting each other for years at a time. Such commitment *"walks the talk."*

"Generally, people talk about so many good things. Their talk is very good, but the walk is not aligned with the talk ... but working particularly for something and providing the particular solution like Duncan is, can transform the world. So I think that walk and talk matched by action and the enthusiasm, the excitement, the commitment, I think that's inspired me about the Acts Community." – Kehkshan.

The conversation with Duncan and Kehkshan affirms that the Acts model is not just history; it is a continuing call. Through Angello and its global partners, that call is being answered with a generosity, shared leadership and sacrificial love that transcends borders and builds lasting impact. The Angello network is not only a professional alliance; it is a spiritual fellowship that mirrors the values lived out in the book of Acts.

Future Vision

Kehkshan Newton envisions a future in which Christian leaders in Pakistan move from the margins to a marketplace where they are not merely participants but pioneers shaping national and global conversations. Her dream is to see a new generation of empowered, faith-driven entrepreneurs who not only build businesses, but also challenge long-standing narratives and systems. This vision of dignity, voice and influence is born from a belief that Christian communities in Pakistan, though small, can become catalysts for transformation and marketplace leadership.

"We have a dream that we can have the generation of Christian leaders who can talk to the global north to recalibrate their thinking patterns." – Kehkshan.

Duncan Parker carries a bold vision for global impact through ethical investment. He believes that even a minor shift in global capital toward purpose-driven businesses — less than 1% of financial assets — could dramatically advance solutions to the world's most pressing social and environmental challenges. His vision challenges investors, institutions and entrepreneurs alike to think beyond profit and mobilize wealth as a force for good, unlocking scalable and sustainable change.

"If you can just convince people with wealth to invest it into doing good, where that money can grow as well… then that's kind of exciting." – Duncan.

Together, Kehkshan and Duncan envision a world where faith, leadership and enterprise converge to create a more just, hopeful, and empowered future both locally and globally.

CLOSING REFLECTIONS

This conversation is a testament to the power of faith, enterprise and community. Through their lived experiences, Kehkshan and Duncan offer a roadmap for entrepreneurs who desire to succeed in business and live a God-given calling with purpose, courage and integrity.

"When Kehkshan used the words 'fresh air,' the word that came to my mind, the picture I got was, that it's about hope ... hope and vision are closely aligned, but actually it's about who you journey with and who you travel with in getting there. And being humble enough to be schooled every single day by, and inspired every single day by, those people. It's not so much about the destination, it's about the journey." – Duncan.

Duncan points out that what really matters along the way is the fellowship, the *"finding your tribe."* Angello calls it a network, and Duncan suggests there's a tribal aspect to it ... *"these are my people."* This doesn't mean you always agree with each other, *"because you need people who challenge you and take you out of your comfort zone."*

Kehkshan reveals that she has learned "the hard way" that God reveals the way forward step by step; that patience and blind trust that the Lord is leading the way is needed. She cautions against wanting to lead the way on your own; it's then that you will discover you want to move fast, but you're not moving in the right direction. Responding to the question of advice to those who are seeking a life driven by God's purposes for them, Kehkshan answers:

"So I think that faith in those steps without losing your patience and keeping your passion level very high ... Because I think passion is the fuel that catalyzes you every day for your purpose in life ... Strongly believe!" – Kehkshan.

Kehkshan shares that the most inspiring thing about Christ is His heroic nature - He changes the situation. She applies this inspiration to life in general.

"If there is a turmoil, change it into something very positive. If there is a sickness, turn it into a healthy life." – Kehkshan.

Her closing reflection is that, at 38 years old, she has seen in Pakistan over the last two decades a reluctance to invest in young leadership. She urges the importance of thinking about the young ones, giving them space to provide momentum to the country.

"You are not the sole owner of everything around you." – Kehkshan.

Kehkshan's advice is grounded in perseverance, faith and a commitment to lifting others out of poverty. She reminds us that impact begins with trust and is sustained by vision, commitment and the willingness to empower the next generation.

Duncan encourages entrepreneurs to surround themselves with a community of truth-tellers, encouragers and believers — those who share the road, refine your purpose, and fuel your hope.

"What's your vision, what's the hope that's within that vision, and who you're going to journey that with?" – Duncan.

Together, the reflections of Kehkshan and Duncan form a powerful call to build boldly, lead faithfully, and to never walk alone.

Obedience with Hakan Sandberg and Manpan Wungak

Introduction

Hakan Sandberg is a passionate Swedish entrepreneur dedicated to fostering growth in individuals and organisations. Hakan is the architect behind Itzinya Networks, a business incubator designed to equip leaders to train and disciple young entrepreneurs in emerging markets and amongst those forcibly displaced across Europe and the Middle East. His innovative franchise model allows locally owned and operated Itzinya Business Centers to work within their own cultural context while connecting through a global network, thereby enabling international synergies, peer mentoring and shared best practice.

Manpan Wungak, a Nigerian trained veterinary doctor, an evangelist, a mentor and an entrepreneur who was searching for effective ways to help young people grow in faith and livelihood, met Hakan Sandberg at a conference and became involved with Itzinya. Since then, for almost a decade, he has been multiplying entrepreneurs in several cities in Nigeria. Manpan was raised in a Christian home and developed *"a deep passion for helping people fulfil their destinies,"* based on his belief that *"those who live may no longer live for themselves but for Him who died for them."* He describes this as his purpose in life, no longer living for himself but for the calling, which is to be a disciple. He has worked with several mission organizations over the years and has been running his own Agri business.

This conversation explores the powerful intersection of faith, entrepreneurship and community transformation. Hakan and Manpan have a shared passion for empowering young people to discover and pursue their God-given purpose through business. Their collaboration through Itzinya has become a model for blending biblical discipleship, marketplace engagement and sustainable development. Their work demonstrates how godly principles can shape business ventures and entire communities. This interview offers rich insights and encouragement for entrepreneurs seeking to integrate faith with work, building ventures that serve both people and purpose with lasting spiritual and practical impact. (*See bios of Hakan and Manpan in Appendix One*).

Leadership and Impact

As a young evangelist Hakan set out to meet "unreached people groups" and spent five years planting churches in Albania, where there was high unemployment in a predominantly young population. His experiences there taught him that if he wanted to reach young people before they decide to emigrate elsewhere, he needed to provide work for them. So he returned to Sweden and immersed himself in business to learn how to create jobs. Thereafter he set out on missions again, but as a businessperson equipped to train potential business leaders.

In 2014 Hakan founded Itzinya (It's-in-you) to assist young entrepreneurs to start, run and grow their own businesses. Itzinya's Mission statement is "*unleashing leaders through training, incubating and accelerating value-driven entrepreneurs with a key focus on transforming the entrepreneurs.*" The foundational values of the company are Hope, Integrity, Dedication and Growth. Their programmes include a Startup Academy which utilises proven start-up tools and processes formatted in practical, accessible workshops; an Accelerator Programme for proven businesses that need scaling, utilising effective processes designed by and for entrepreneurs; and a Leadership Programme that trains leaders to unlock potential through service and facilitation, developing trust, and improving character and competence.

Manpan learnt from his early evangelising efforts that to

become involved with young people it's necessary to be relevant in their lives. This led him to explore entrepreneurship development. Together with Bible studies, Manpan tried to help young people interested in business to succeed in what they were trying to do. He met Hakan at a conference after Hakan had overheard him explaining to someone how he was trying to help young people find purpose in life through business. Manpan describes that moment as "*a turning point*" in his life.

"*I was doing it without any such tools or road map or any processes. I was just free styling, groping my way in the dark, trying to find what works and what doesn't. And then it turns out, Hakan had already developed these tools and processes that would help make my work easier. And so we connected on that. And in 2016 he was brave enough to make the journey to Nigeria to help us launch Itzinya in Nigeria.*" – Manpan.

Itzinya has been operating in Nigeria for 10 years now, and Manpan describes it as being the "*turning point*" in the lives of many. Manpan explains that Itzinya has a Godly purpose - they are not just helping people to start businesses, they are helping them to connect with the "*true meaning of life, which is their calling to be in Christ.*"

Hakan's model for Itzinya ensures that it is about building structures that multiply impact sustainably. Hakan relates that before Itzinya became properly established, they focused on "*unreached groups*" and young people in emerging markets. Then came the war in Syria, and many Syrian refugees fled to Sweden. This gave Hakan the opportunity to test the concept at home. He confesses to how surprised he was at how well it worked. The market in Sweden is so advanced that he had wondered how a person from Syria could successfully start a business there. It turned out that the principles behind starting a business were all that was needed, because there was a ready-made market of refugees and migrants which Swedish people were not equipped to tap into. That led to the company spreading into Europe. They now work with migrants and refugees in Europe and with young people in emerging markets such as Manpan's franchise in Nigeria and further afield, including Central and Southeast Asia, Pakistan and some countries we cannot mention due to security issues.

It is clear from this conversation that Hakan leads with humility and intentionality to release others to lead. His spiritual vison has led to transferring tools for others to replicate so that they can achieve success.

"To create sustainability is also to create dignity. To create dignity where it is not about us helping you, but it's more like you have everything that you need." – Hakan.

Manpan's leadership exemplifies servanthood, perseverance and relational depth. His Itzinya team in Nigeria has successfully guided over 20 cohorts of aspiring entrepreneurs and started around 150 businesses. His approach is relational and deeply grounded in Christ-centred mentorship to help young people discover both their purpose in Christ and their capacity to contribute economically and spiritually to their communities. His impact is visible not only in the ventures launched, but also in the lives transformed through character formation and spiritual growth.

"It's not what I know or what I do, but what God can do through what I am." – Manpan.

Together, Hakan and Manpan offer a powerful model of collaborative, faith-driven leadership, combining global systems thinking with local, relational action. Their partnership in business and discipleship reflects a leadership style that is spiritually rooted, strategic and empowering.

Challenges and Lessons

In nurturing faith-driven ventures through Itzinya, Hakan and Manpan have encountered numerous spiritual, relational and practical challenges. Their responses in this interview offer valuable lessons for any entrepreneur working in cross-cultural or under-resourced contexts.

Manpan highlights consideration of context as a key lesson. When they started, they assumed that if they applied the principles, businesses would emerge. What they didn't consider was that these young entrepreneurs had opted for businesses training for purposes of survival. Joblessness was endemic, so buying and selling at a small profit was a way to survive. But if a job opportunity came up, they took it. Manpan and his team would spend three to four years coaching potential business owners only to find that when offered a job, they abandoned the business.

"... context matters; understand the environment you're working in." - Manpan

"So that was the first shock ... we needed to think about those questions when we interacted with entrepreneurs." – Manpan.

They also learnt that not every business had the same impact on society, so they began to prioritise businesses that were scalable in both financial viability and social impact by creating jobs in the local community. Social impact became a key metric, alongside sustainability. Further, Manpan and his team learnt that "mindset shift takes a while." It is unrealistic to assume that once people learn something new, they will quickly change their minds and their habits.

"I realized that people have to unlearn things that they grew up with and then learn new things ... the concept of accountability, and also the concept of saving or investing." – Manpan.

Manpan and his team discovered it was necessary to encourage entrepreneurs to think beyond themselves and consider not only personal gain, but also how their work contributes to wider transformation. Manpan explains that in most of the African cultures, Nigeria in particular, there is no word for investment. Instead of investing profit to expand the business, they would spend it. It was necessary to teach people to differentiate between business money and personal money; that is, to draw a percentage of the profits as earnings but ensure that the rest goes into growing the business. Manpan found the most effective way to convey the principles of saving and investment was to describe spending as "killing" money, which actually is what the word "spending" means in their language.

"So you need to help people to understand ... spending money is killing money. So you kill the money. Anything that you kill, unfortunately, would have no part in the future.." – Manpan.

Manpan reveals that it has been a continual process of adapting to the lessons learnt in the local context, and their focus has shifted from teaching theoretical business principles to more contextual, human-centred coaching. Teaching concepts like investment, saving, accountability and sustainability revealed deep-rooted cultural and systemic barriers. And they have learnt that changing how people think about money, trust and long-term planning requires patience, empathy and repetition. Financial behaviour is shaped by worldview, not only knowledge.

Hakan places great store in the value of fellowship and collaboration. He loves to be with his partners doing the certification training and meeting people in new countries and different contexts, particular those 'on fire' for serving young people, such as Manpan. Collaboration provides insights into best practice learnt from the hard experiences of others, and this has prepared the ground for a thorough training programme. The secret to the success of the franchise like structure was ensuring everything was well prepared to help franchisees deliver a high-quality product, and this has added great leverage to the business to sustain and multiply the good that they wanted to do.

Above all, Hakan regards servanthood and humility as the key values for a business to cultivate. He comments that many young people coming into business are preoccupied with themselves and their great idea, convinced people are going to love it and they are going to make money. He reminds us that "business is a very simple concept, because it is about serving people." It requires empathy.

"When you start to walk in the shoes of your customer - really get to know who they are, where they live, what their life is about, what the pain is that they feel, why they need a solution - then you can start to build a solution that actually speaks to them." – Hakan.

Hakan points out that continually talking with customers and becoming fully familiar with their circumstances is the route to finding solutions that will address their problems. Then, when the solution emerges, they will feel it has been designed solely for them and that will bring longevity to the relationship, thereby improving the sustainability of your business. Service, says Hakan, is loving your neighbour in a tangible way that will help their lives. The route to a thriving business is to attract customers by identifying their top priority - that which they care enough about to spend their money on. There is a correspondence between simple business principles and righteous purpose, and such purpose comes from the heart, not the head.

The greatest life lesson Hakan imparts in this conversation is that God's will is paramount, and our role is obedience.

"It is not about me. It is about what God wants. Is not about my kingdom. It's about his kingdom. In the ups and downs, which is part of business life … you can feel so many times that, well, this is impossible, or I don't have any more in me to do this. Then it has been important for me to remember that I am responsible for obedience, not for results."

Hakan voices the counterintuitive revelation that although

impact may be your valid purpose, it should not be your focus.

"So the stubbornness or the grit that we're talking about, the passion and perseverance for long term goals, how do you have that? How can you have that? What is motivating you to have that? And I would say (although) it is about the results, the impact, if you like, that is not my focus, because I cannot squeeze the fruit out of the tree. My part is the obedience to (do) what I know is right and when I know I'm called to do it." – Hakan.

He uses the metaphor of the fruit tree to emphasize that so often we are in such a hurry to see the fruit that we pull it up with the roots to see if there is anything alive in there.

"But, over time, if we are obedient to what we know is right, the fruit comes naturally, and it's a lifetime journey." – Hakan.

Challenges have not weakened the resolve of Hakan and Manpan. To the contrary, challenges have shaped their character, helped them refine their model, and strengthened their faith.

Key Themes and Insights

Calling and Context: From Ministry to Marketplace: Both Hakan and Manpan were drawn into entrepreneurship not out of personal ambition, but through a deep desire to serve others and live out their faith in practical ways. Hakan's early work in church planting in Albania exposed a major gap: Spiritual growth was not enough without economic empowerment.
"If I want to reach young people and I want them to be able to establish God's Kingdom locally and spread, I need to be able to provide work for them." – Hakan

Manpan, rooted in discipleship and community leadership, began to see business as a more effective way to help young people discover purpose and live for Christ. Their shared insight was clear: Business could become both mission and ministry.

Faith as Foundation: For both men, faith is not an accessory to their work; it is the driving force and moral compass for everything they do. Their ventures are built on the biblical principles of stewardship, service, dignity and obedience to God. This faith-based grounding gives their work meaning beyond profit and defines how they lead, serve, and build.

"We don't do it because we want to make more money ... we do it because there is an eternal value to what we do" – Manpan.

Empowerment Through Business: At the heart of their mission is the belief that entrepreneurship is a tool for restoring dignity, unlocking purpose, and empowering communities. Through the Itzinya Networks, Hakan and Manpan train young people not only in business principles and method but also in mindset change, helping them to grow in confidence, independence, self-discipline and spiritual maturity. In this way, business becomes a context for both economic sustainability and personal discipleship.

"It is not about us helping you, but it's more like you have everything that you need." – Hakan.

The Power of Unlikely Partnerships: Hakan and Manpan's collaboration is a striking example of cross-cultural, cross-continental partnership. Hakan, from Sweden, and Manpan, from Nigeria, represent different backgrounds and experiences, yet they found common ground in a shared purpose to raise up Godly entrepreneurs. Their partnership is built on humility, trust and mutual learning, recognizing that the Spirit of God is at work everywhere and that the best solutions are co-created, not imposed.

Business as Worship: Hakan and Manpan believe that entrepreneurship can be an act of worship when practised with integrity, purpose and service at its core. Business, when aligned with God's values, becomes a sacred space where love, creativity and justice meet real-world needs. This mindset reshapes the role of the Christian entrepreneur from wealth creator to kingdom ambassador.

"If we can translate our following of Jesus, the values … the new life that Jesus gives, the generosity that he has shown us … I believe that work becomes an excellent way of worshiping." – Hakan.

Loving the Problem, Not Just the Solution: One of the greatest lessons Hakan shares is about truly understanding the pain points of the people you serve. Many entrepreneurs start with a product idea instead of listening deeply to the needs around them. By focusing on the problem and not rushing to push a solution they help entrepreneurs build ventures that matter.

"The longest journey is from my head to the head of the customer, from my heart to the heart of the customer." – Hakan.

Transformation Takes Time: Whether shifting mindsets around money, challenging cultural norms, or discipling young people into a kingdom worldview, both leaders emphasize patience, consistency, and grace. True transformation is rarely quick, but it is always worth it.

"So we are in a hurry to see the fruit come out, and we're squeezing and we're pulling up the tree with the roots to see if something is alive there. But, but over time, if we are obedient to what we know is right, the fruit comes naturally, and it's a lifetime journey." – Hakan.

Key Principles for Faith-Driven Entrepreneurs

1. Obedience Over Outcomes

Success in faith-driven entrepreneurship begins with obedience to God's call, not a fixation on measurable outcomes. This mindset keeps entrepreneurs grounded in trust, patience, and long-term faithfulness, especially when progress is slow or unclear. Obedience is an act of worship, not a strategy for control.

"Jesus brought glory to His Father through obeying; we are bringing glory to Jesus through following him and being like him." - Hakan

"I am responsible for obedience, not for results." – Hakan.

2. Work as Worship

Faith-driven entrepreneurs recognize that their labour is sacred. Business is not separate from spirituality; it is a context in which believers can serve others, steward resources and honour God through excellence, integrity and service.

"Work is where we spend most of our lives ... to be a follower of Jesus needs to be translated into everything that we do. But since work is such a big part of our lives ... I believe that work becomes an excellent way of worshiping" - Hakan.

3. Authentic Fellowship

At the heart of the collaboration between Hakan and Manpan is transparency, humility and shared purpose. They openly share struggles and victories, building a culture of honesty and trust that allows for mutual growth and support. Their leadership style is deeply relational, grounded in a posture of listening, learning and faith-fuelled encouragement.

4. Love the Problem, Not the Solution

Entrepreneurship isn't about pushing a product; it's about solving real problems. This requires empathy, humility and deep listening. Faith-driven leaders are called to serve, designing solutions that reflect genuine care for people's struggles, not just market demand.

"When you love the problem, you have to dig into your customer ... when you start to walk in the shoes of your customer, really get to know who they are." – Hakan.

5. Context Matters

In many regions, especially emerging markets, people launch businesses out of survival, not strategic opportunity. Understanding this reshapes how mentors, investors and supporters engage with entrepreneurs, bringing compassion, relevance and patience to the process.

Effective leaders adapt their approach to the unique realities and motivations of those they serve, rather than imposing generic models of success.

6. Transform Mindsets, Not Just Skills

Entrepreneurial growth is as much about internal transformation as it is about external tools. Lasting change often comes through renewed thinking about money, trust, responsibility, and vision. The mind-shift towards saving and investing and wisely embracing accountability and long-term planning takes time, but is essential for building resilient, purpose-driven businesses.

7. Keep an Eternal Perspective

Faith-driven entrepreneurs lead with humility and dependency on God, knowing that their identity and impact are not ultimately defined by business metrics. Their work carries eternal significance, and their posture reflects trust in what God is doing in them and through them, even beyond what they can see.

Reflections on the Angello Network and the Acts Community Values

The obedience to their calling that Hakan and Manpan reveal reflects the very heart of the Angello network. Their commitment to faith-integrated entrepreneurship and cross-cultural fellowship brings stories that empower and equip. Their partnership, built on mutual respect and a shared Kingdom vision, aligns deeply with Angello's mission to elevate voices from emerging markets and build unity through purpose-driven collaboration.

Hakan's approach to his working life is grounded in his belief that "to be a follower of Jesus needs to be translated into everything that we do." He is acutely conscious of the generous gift of new life through Jesus and believes that since we spend much of our lives working, we are called to bring glory to God through our work.

Hakan sees business as a place where "the gospel gets flesh." To serve God through serving a network of customers and other stakeholders is showing love in action. It is more powerful than charitable aid because enabling people to become self-sufficient through entrepreneurship creates dignity. Business is not merely economic; it has a spiritual purpose. Hakan views the marketplace as a sacred space where believers express love, embody service and advance the gospel through excellence, self-giving and faithfulness.

"Love is a verb and should be expressed in what we do and how we provide for people ... business is far better than giving gifts. That has its place. But to create sustainability is also to create dignity. And ... that is one very, very important thing, especially when we work with this big gap between rich and poor in the world that we have today." – Hakan.

In high-impact, high-demand work, burnout is a real risk. Hakan emphasizes the importance of spiritual rhythm, fellowship and collaboration as keys to sustainability. Staying rooted in God's presence and in a community of peers allows Hakan and Manpan to continue leading with vision and strength, without losing joy or perspective.

"People like us are doers. We're hard wired to do, do, do, and we can burn out by just keep doing. We see that the combination of being and doing, having that flow back and forth all the time between drawing back to the Lord, remembering where we come from, remembering what's really important in life, and then, from the strength of being with God, go out and do the things that we are called to do." – Hakan.

Fellowship and collaboration with like-minded leaders who practise the flow of action and contemplation enables resilience and sustainability. The rhythm of being and doing, of purposeful activity through spending time with God and remaining obedient, prevents burnout and ensures that action flows from intimacy, not striving.

That balance, that sustainability that comes from encouraging one another in what we call Acts Communities, to be together … is something that I believe will up our game totally and make us sustainable and have impact in the long term." – Hakan.

Through all their challenges they have seen God's provision and have become stronger, more resilient leaders.

"This, for us, is a real journey of faith, and it has opened our eyes to see what God can do if you're willing to walk the distance and endure the challenges along the way." – Manpan. Through the Angello network Hakan and Manpan have found encouragement, connection and the validation of shared purpose, knowing they are not alone in the work of integrating faith and enterprise for transformative impact.

"Talent is equally distributed, but opportunity is not … if we can provide opportunity for people, then most of the job is

done because the energy and the ingenuity and the invention is what's spread all over God's creation." – Hakan.

Their work mirrors Angello's vision of walking side by side with leaders in diverse contexts, empowering them to build with dignity, competence and calling. In doing so, they affirm that the future of entrepreneurship - and the Church — rests in shared stories, distributed leadership and Spirit-led innovation.

The spirit of Acts 2: 42–47, of fellowship, shared purpose, service and transformation, is embedded in how Hakan and Manpan lead and build. Itzinya operates as a Kingdom franchise where tools, training and wisdom are shared for multiplication of impact. The model prioritizes local leadership, allowing communities to flourish with dignity. The Itzinya approach fosters networks of support through peer groups, mentorship structures and shared journeys that emphasize accountability and encouragement. Entrepreneurs should not walk alone; they flourish in the context of relational, faith-driven community.

Everything Itzinya does is directed toward spiritual and social renewal. Whether training a new entrepreneur or developing systems across continents, their posture remains one of service, not status. They lead with open hands and hearts, empowering others to rise. Together, Hakan and Manpan embody the essence of a modern-day Acts Community. They are authentic, generous, faith-fuelled, and committed to seeing the Kingdom expressed in both word and deed through lives and businesses rooted in Christ.

Future Vision

Looking ahead, Hakan and Manpan share a bold and hope-filled vision for the role of entrepreneurship in the global Church and society. Their outlook is shaped by a deep belief in the power of business to transform lives, communities and even spiritual ecosystems.
Both men see the marketplace as a primary arena for gospel

impact in the years to come. As traditional church structures face new challenges, the workplace is emerging as a vital space where believers can live out their faith in practical, transformative ways. Entrepreneurs are not only economic players, they are missionaries, culture-shapers and discipleship leaders, advancing God's Kingdom through innovation, service and stewardship. Hakan believes that entrepreneurial leadership will become increasingly essential to the Church and to society. As structures evolve and communities seek new expressions of faith, it is adaptable, visionary, entrepreneurs who should lead the way. They are not only creating jobs and businesses; they are building networks of faith, accountability and service that look remarkably like the early church.

"… as entrepreneurial people (we) are finding solutions to things … ploughing the way for new things, building new structures, new movements. I think that into the future, the role of entrepreneurs, not just in the marketplace, but also in in the church … will be important; we are important contributors to find new ways to establish new structures that are important for the future. So I think in a time where everything is so up and down, there's so much change, we need to take our place and take our role in that and contribute with the gifts that we have been given." – Hakan.

Thanks to digital technology, virtual tools and easier international mobility, geographical and cultural lines are blurring. The gospel is no longer confined by nation or tradition; it is moving fluidly across regions and professions.

"The lines are disappearing. Previously, you wouldn't imagine having a conversation with someone in Sweden or South Africa or elsewhere. But the lines are disappearing, both because of technology and also the fact that we travel more nowadays. So we interact more with one another, and we get each other's perspective nowadays. I think that opens the door for opportunity. It also opens the door for the gospel to be more mobile in the nations." – Manpan.

This mobility creates unprecedented opportunities for intercontinental and cross-continental partnerships in which faith-driven entrepreneurs from different backgrounds can co-create solutions for shared challenges. The Itzinya network, originally developed in Sweden, is now taking root in Africa, Central Asia, and beyond. Their model of combining business incubation with discipleship is adaptable across cultures, meeting people where they are and equipping them to build where they live. With a scalable structure and a spiritually grounded ethos, Itzinya is poised to become a global tool for economic and spiritual renewal, multiplying leaders who multiply impact.

Hakan and Manpan envision a future where faith and entrepreneurship are not parallel tracks but deeply integrated paths to purpose, transformation and Kingdom advancement.

Closing Reflections

This conversation with Hakan Sandberg and Manpan Wungak is a powerful reminder that business rooted in faith and service can become a vehicle for deep and long-lasting transformation. Their lives and leadership exemplify what it means to walk in obedience to God, building ventures that prioritize people over profit, and trusting that fruitfulness comes in God's time.

Whether you are just beginning the entrepreneurial journey or seeking to realign your current work with eternal purpose, their stories invite you to:

- Pursue purpose beyond profit
- Build in community, not isolation
- Serve faithfully, trusting God with the results

Their partnership paints a compelling portrait of faithful, purpose-driven entrepreneurship — a model not just for business, but for calling, character and Kingdom impact. It is a call to sow faithfully, love deeply, and lead with humility, believing that the work done in faith will ripple far beyond what we can see today.

"I see there is a yearning for more, beyond just making money and just living a good life; there is a yearning for more, and people are asking themselves, 'What is the purpose in all of this?' And I think that … is what gives me hope more than anything else."" – Manpan.

"We're underestimating what we can do in a lifetime, and we're totally overestimating what we can do in a short while." – Hakan.

Justice with Nikolaus Hutter and Edson Niwamanya

Introduction

This conversation with **Nikolaus Hutter** and **Edson Niwamanya** offers a compelling insight into the intersection of purpose and entrepreneurship within emerging markets and what Nikolaus calls *"the blind spots - the people, places and topics that markets neglect."* As key figures in Relevant Ventures, a purpose-driven venture catalyst, their partnership bridges continents. Nikolaus and Edson come from vastly different worlds. Nikolaus is an Austrian economist and investor shaped by global finance, and Edson is a Ugandan entrepreneur raised in humble conditions. Yet their lives converged through a shared commitment to justice and purpose-driven impact.

Nikolaus Hutter is based in Vienna, and has lived and worked in several countries. His academic specialisation is institutional and behavioural economics, studying the collective and individual laws, beliefs, and customs that drive individual and collective behaviours. For the last 15 years he has focused on impact investment and social enterprises, which he prefers to call 'purpose-driven business and investment,' because its purpose reaches beyond making money and solving economic problems – it requires holistic consideration of all the systems that shape choice, including society, ecology, and spirituality. The quintuple bottom line of purpose-driven business and investment is purpose, profit, people, planet and place – i.e.: financial sustainability, social inclusion, environmental regeneration, security and safety, and moral and spiritual elevation. Nikolaus is the co-founder, with two others, of Relevant Ventures, a purpose-venture catalyst that empowers entrepreneurs through enterprise and investment solutions to address humanitarian and planetary crisis.

Edson Niwamanya is based in Kampala, Uganda. Soon after he left school Edson became involved with the Social Innovation Academy (SINA), which trains young people to start social businesses that will create social change in their local contexts. Inspired by his grandfather, a man of deep faith and the first in his family to be educated, Edson launched a project to bring entrepreneurial leadership and character development into Ugandan schools. He went on to work with incubators, both globally and internationally, as a business mentor, drawing from his own entrepreneurial journey Edson has recently attained a bachelor's degree in entrepreneurial leadership from the African Leadership University.

It was at SINA that Edson met Nikolaus. In 2021, having been *"very well mentored"* in finance by Nikolaus and the team at SINA, Edson was invited to join their financial solution concept, the Purpose Pool, designed to close the financing gap for entrepreneurs looking for capital between $5000 to $50,000. This proved very successful and led to the founding of Relevant Ventures. Together, Edson and Nikolaus are building ventures that address systemic challenges while embodying purpose principles and a shared commitment to justice, equity, and spiritual integrity. Their collaboration reflects how purpose-driven fellowship and practical entrepreneurship can co-create impactful solutions that serve both people and planet.

This interview explores the origins of their partnership, the ventures they have launched, and the spiritual and operational principles that guide their work, offering rich insights for anyone seeking to lead with purpose in complex, dynamic contexts. (*See bios of Nikolaus and Edson in Appendix One*)

Leadership and Impact

A hallmark of Nikolaus' approach to leadership and impact is identifying ventures that *"should exist but don't"* — solutions that respond to real needs yet are overlooked by traditional systems. Whether it's unlocking rooftop solar opportunities in overlooked institutions or integrating renewable energy into school nutrition programs, Nikolaus brings a systems-thinking mindset to every challenge.

Nikolaus describes the work of Relevant Ventures as financial *"plumbing"* - channelling liquidity where it ought to go but currently doesn't. By doing so, they are building ventures that should exist but don't. Their focus is on the *"blind spots,"* the people, places, and topics too often ignored. For Nikolaus, these blind spots are not peripheral but central to the great turning point humanity now faces. He explains that their work is about *"developing and building business and investment solutions to address humanitarian and planetary crises."* He uses the word *"crisis"* not only in the modern sense of a potential disaster, but also in its original Greek sense of a *"turning point,"* where a choice must be made between *"this way or that."*

"As humanity ... a global community ... we are at a turning point, and we need to make a choice, whether we go this way or that way. The way of freedom, rule of law, democracy, solidarity and belief in science or a darker way ... and every activity and almost every choice, every moment today, I think, needs to be, at some point in reflection, framed in that framing of crisis, of turning point, of making choices." – Nikolaus.

Every venture, every choice, Nikolaus argues, must ultimately be framed in this context of responsible decision-making.

Nikolaus' leadership is marked by humility, reflection, and sensitive intuition. He avoids the term *"vision,"* regarding it as somewhat *"self-glorious."* Rather, venture building starts with *"a process of sensing, of seeing things,"* of developing an ability to *"put yourself in the way of opportunity."* Having accumulated 25 years of experience, first as a finance professional, then as a private equity consultant doing commercial due diligence, and now as a venture capital investor, Nicolaus simplifies his current role as anticipating *"where the ball bounces the second time."* This metaphor, drawn from Ronald Cohen's book 'The Second Bounce of the

Ball', speaks to the fact that although initial decision-making is under some degree of personal control - "*you can actually throw it there*"- the real challenge is to anticipate "*where it bounces, especially if the ground is rocky.*" Nikolaus argues that it's possible to cultivate this ability: "*It's a muscle you can train.*"

During years of capacity building through a variety of entrepreneurship empowerment programmes Nikolaus and his team have "*stumbled across*" opportunities that they sensed could work and have explored ways to make them do so.

"What we're quite good at is not just seeing that, but finding ways to make it work, right? And then we call that 'the angels in the detail' … once you start digging into something, you find lots of treasure." – Nikolaus.

Nikolaus explains that the "*angels in the detail*" emerge when you start thinking, talking and really understanding the needs of your partners. It is then that "*business and finance go to power,*" says Nikolaus. He cites by way of example the knock-on effect of socially advantageous partnerships that can emerge by applying one's mind to the enterprise potential in solarizing roof spaces for NGOs such as the Red Cross, or Catholic schools in Uganda

"It's this re-purposing of business and of finance that really makes the difference, but the more meaningful the purpose, the more powerful the energy that you release." – Nikolaus.

Nikolaus declares that the mission of Relevant Ventures is to accelerate the shift to a purpose-drive economy, not through activism or lamenting that such a world does not yet exist, but through building viable businesses that work because they can see the potential for good and put themselves "*in the way of opportunities.*"

Edson Niwamanya's energetic and empathetic leadership

style was obvious at a young age, demonstrated in his first enterprise to help young people in school develop character and social entrepreneurial awareness. His mentoring work with local and global incubators reinforced his passion for empowering others. Although Edson had no formal background in the finance sector, Nikolaus and his team invested in his potential by tutoring him in finance. Between 2021 and 2023, Edson grew to lead the Purpose Pool's investment activities, deploying $110,000 into ten early-stage social businesses. These enterprises created more than 140 jobs, grew significantly, and went on to attract nearly $300,000 in additional capital. The success of these investments reinforced Edson's conviction that addressing the financing gap could unlock exponential impact. This work among them, laid the foundations for Relevant Ventures.

Today, Edson continues to shape Relevant Ventures' approach to investing in overlooked entrepreneurs. He tells of how they are investing in Ugandan social entrepreneurs who are *"doing amazing work, from producing mosquito repellent products to fight malaria, to enabling coffee farmers receive competitive prices for their coffee."* He regards Relevant Ventures' role as that of an enabler, by investing right and demonstrating the opportunities. In collaboration with SIEMENS Foundation, they pruduced research on the problem of access to finance. The research reveals the reality of the finance gap, but it also shows there are solutions to the problem. Through their pilot programmes they have case studies which demonstrate that by identifying a problem and using whatever limited resources they had, their entrepreneurial partners found solutions. The story to be told, says Edson, is that "people have purpose" and are worth investing in.

"We all are doing something for a reason, and I think our contribution is to see, to do and to inspire ... our mission is to lead and be the example ... to inspire others to move on the same path of creating this purpose economy." – Edson.

Edson's leadership is rooted in the community values of his

culture, embodying the principles of servant leadership. His aim is a just society, and he leads from an intrinsic desire to empower others through mentorship, partnership, and presence. His story highlights the power of justice-driven entrepreneurship. It also demonstrates the impact of the mentorship afforded to him, in which Nikolaus played a pivotal role in equipping him with the tools and confidence to grow into his current role as an investment professional serving emerging and overlooked markets.

Together, Nikolaus and Edson model transformational leadership, uniting technical excellence with purpose, humility, insight and grounded, people-centred implementation. Their partnership stands as a powerful example of what's possible when leadership is both globally informed and locally rooted.

Challenges and Lessons

Nikolaus and Edson speak candidly about the realities of working in emerging markets, offering not only a clear-eyed view of the obstacles but also the wisdom and faith required to navigate them. Their reflections reveal important lessons for entrepreneurs working across cultural and contextual boundaries.

Operating in markets like Uganda comes with unique challenges, such as businesses lacking formal registration, limited access to infrastructure and unfamiliarity with bureaucratic systems. These are not mere inconveniences but fundamental realities that require a shift in mindset and method. Rather than applying rigid Western business templates, successful entrepreneurs in these contexts must lead with empathy, curiosity and humility, co-creating solutions that are appropriate and sustainable.

Rather than calling these realities "challenges," Edson describes them as "uncertainties" — conditions that require resilience, creativity, and adaptability. This has been particularly evident in early-stage investing, where the definition of "early stage" is radically different from that in Europe, the U.S., or even neighbouring African countries. To work effectively in such an environment requires curiosity, patience, and what Edson calls *"eye-level collaboration"* amongst stakeholders, from entrepreneurs and local leaders to governments, peer organizations, and investors.

In practice, this means recognizing that what might be considered standard elsewhere, such as business registration or formal record-keeping, cannot be assumed in Uganda. Many entrepreneurs operate without registration, not out of negligence but because the process is complex, inaccessible, or poorly understood. To an external investor, this might look like failure; to Edson, it reflects structural and knowledge barriers that must be navigated with empathy.

By embracing the uniqueness of the Ugandan context and meeting it with humility, empathy and partnership, Edson and the Relevant Ventures team have been able to build financing models and mentoring approaches that actually work for entrepreneurs on the ground. Edson's perspective is shaped by this local context. He resists labels like "third world," preferring to see Uganda as a context with its own unique mix of *"opportunities and uncertainties."* Success, he insists, comes from embracing that uniqueness rather than imposing outside models.

His reflections serve as a reminder that emerging and strife-torn markets demand more than financial capital; they demand the ability to co-create solutions in step with those closest to the local reality.

"If you bring the mindset from Europe or US or elsewhere where these things are expected to be there, and you impose them on a market like ours, you're not going to create any kind of impact. You will pack your bags and go back home."
– Edson.

Nikolaus builds on this perspective, noting that in *"raw"*

environments where safety nets are few and risks are visible, there is a kind of honest exposure which teaches that resilience, community solidarity and lived vulnerability foster strength, connectedness, and resourcefulness.

He encourages those from more comfortable contexts to immerse themselves in such environments for their own growth. Rejecting the paternalistic mindset of pity that too often frames Western view of Africa, Nikolaus argues that the learning curve flows *"the other way."* Drawing from his experiences in Burkina Faso and Uganda, and in hotspots such as the Balkans and Ukraine, he highlights four interlinked lessons that *"raw humanity"* contexts reveal with clarity:

1. **Risk perception.** Exposure to uncertainty teaches people to discern risks. In contexts where threats are visible and unavoidable, there is less illusion of safety and more grounded wisdom about what truly matters. Systemic shocks like COVID-19 or the subprime financial crisis reveal that the greatest dangers are often those unseen, particularly from a context of comfort.

2. **Connectedness of systems.** Every system is only as resilient as its most vulnerable parts. Building resilience requires engaging with and strengthening those most exposed, whether they be vulnerable communities in Africa, neglected Roma settlements in Europe, or refugee camps across the world. Ignoring these *"weak links"* undermines the whole.

3. **Blind spots.** Markets and societies consistently overlook people, places, and problems considered marginal, yet these are often where both need and wisdom converge most profoundly. Confronting blind spots demands humility, openness, and a willingness to learn from the edges.

4. **Solidarity and community as real wealth.** In contexts of scarcity and exposure, solidarity, reciprocity and belonging are not optional but essential for survival. These dynamics generate what Nikolaus calls *"virtuous cycles"*: The more

one is dependent upon others, the more one cannot afford arrogance or cruelty. Reliance on community fosters humility, which in turn cultivates meaningful relationships and growth into one's best personal self. *"Real wealth"* is measured not in accumulation but in connection, character and contribution.

Nikolaus emphasizes how these lessons are deeply interconnected: Risk perception sharpens awareness of vulnerability, vulnerability compels solidarity, and solidarity fosters relational and spiritual flourishing.

"You can't be mean to others if you rely on them." – Nikolaus.

For Nikolaus, to be immersed in such environments is a privilege: *"It makes me feel very alive and very human,"* he reflects. Western societies often insulate themselves from risk through borders, wealth, or gated living, but in doing so, they isolate themselves from the richness of community solidarity, humility and spiritual depth.

"In the end, the last shirt doesn't have any pockets ... What matters is, 'Have I had a life filled with meaningful relationships of love and appreciation and respect?' ... and *"Have I had the chance to be my best personal self, intellectually but also relationally?'"* – Nikolaus.

Rather than insulating themselves from risk, purpose-driven entrepreneurs are called to engage with risk redemptively, building structures that uplift the most vulnerable and strengthen the whole.

Together, Edson and Nikolaus illustrate two dimensions of the same lesson. Edson shows how the practical uncertainties of Uganda demand empathy, collaboration, and resilience. Nikolaus shows how the existential realities of *"raw"* contexts reveal deeper truths about risk, community, and human flourishing. Both perspectives reinforce the conviction that purpose-driven entrepreneurs should approach uncertainty not as a barrier, but as a pathway to greater justice, solidarity and impact.

Key Themes and Insights

The Power of Unlikely Partnerships: Nikolaus and Edson's partnership exemplifies how values and purpose can bridge generational, cultural and geographic divides. What began as a mentoring relationship has become a co-creative partnership grounded in shared vision and mutual respect.

"A little boy born here in Uganda, having this big vision and meeting people who share the same values, for me, was very significant." – Edson.

Seeing the Blind Spots: A core theme in their work is addressing what Nikolaus calls "the blind spots" — the people, places and topics that conventional markets ignore. Their ventures deliberately seek out these neglected areas to bring about meaningful transformation.

"We are developing and building business and investment solutions to address humanitarian and planetary crises." – Nikolaus.

Mutual Learning and Eye-Level Collaboration: Nikolaus and Edson's relationship is not based on hierarchy, but on walking side-by-side. Edson emphasizes that true partnership comes from respecting the lived experience and local knowledge of entrepreneurs and communities.

"As humans, we are all good. We're all pursuing something better and bigger than ourselves." - Edson

Purpose as a Multi-Dimensional Force: For Nikolaus and Edson, purpose is not limited to financial success. Their framework includes five bottom lines: Financial sustainability, social inclusion, environmental regeneration, safety and security, and spiritual elevation.

This holistic approach guides their venture building—solutions that are not only viable economically but also healing, socially and spiritually.

"And I think it's all about starting where you are through your story, with your individual story, with your individual purpose, and challenging yourself to make a contribution. It could be through a community group. It could be through a visit to Uganda, it could be through anything, and it's our duty to pursue our biggest purpose." – Edson.

Spiritual Conviction as a Foundation for Innovation: Both men are deeply motivated by their purpose. For Edson, faith is a family legacy and a compass; for Nikolaus, it was a revelatory moment in Burkina Faso that redirected his context of privilege to a higher calling. Their shared belief is that humans are spiritual beings, and this spiritual dimension belongs at the centre of economic and social transformation, not at the margins.

"Humans, in my conviction, are spiritual animals." – Nikolaus.

Turning Constraints into Creativity: Edson's work in Uganda illustrates how constraints such as lack of infrastructure, formal registration or regulatory clarity are opportunities to innovate. These environments demand empathy, relational resourcefulness, and adaptation.

"So you might come expecting infrastructure to be there ... but it is not the case. I think working in this context has equipped me with the resilience, with the curiosity, to be able to find and create the answers where they are." – Edson.

"When it comes to working in emerging markets, I think you have to come with an open mind. And then you need to work at an eye level, and there needs to be a lot of collaboration, and I think that's what has enabled us to learn and build something that actually works for us." - Edson

Entrepreneurship as a Form of Justice: Both believe that entrepreneurship can be a tool for systemic justice. By investing in overlooked entrepreneurs and enabling them to grow, they create not just jobs, but dignity, agency and long-term solutions to local problems affecting health, nutrition, education and lack of access to life-giving resources.

"The more meaningful the purpose, the more powerful the energy that you release." – Nikolaus.

Catalyzing a Purpose-Driven Economy: Ultimately, the mission of both men is to accelerate a global shift to a purpose-driven economy. Rather than merely critiquing the current system, they're building alternatives through entrepreneurship. Profit-driven motives build an atomistic society which is spiritually bereft of social capital.

"What we forget is that we also isolate ourselves and we lose the real world, which is the social capital, the connectedness of being a part of humanity, the spiritual experience of being part of something much bigger, a community, a tribe, a movement, a circle of friendship." – Nikolaus.

Key Principles for Purpose-Driven Entrepreneurs

1. Purpose Beyond Profit

For Nikolaus and Edson, entrepreneurship is not merely about generating income; it's about creating holistic impact. They champion a quintuple bottom line of:

- Financial sustainability
- Social inclusion
- Environmental regeneration
- Safety and security
- Spiritual elevation

This framework challenges conventional business metrics by ensuring ventures contribute to the common good across multiple dimensions. As Nikolaus puts it, this is about "*repurposing business and finance*" to justly serve humanity and the planet.

2. Start Where You Are

Edson's journey is a testament to beginning with what you have and where you are. From rural Uganda, he launched initiatives rooted in his community's needs and eventually built internationally recognized impact. His advice is simple yet profound:

"It's all about starting where you are through your story, with your individual story, with your individual purpose." – Edson.

3. Purpose as a Catalyst

Edson attributes much of his drive and vision to the faith legacy of his grandfather, whose belief in education transformed generations. Nikolaus describes a pivotal church trip to Burkina Faso where a local leader reshaped his view of justice, dignity and leadership. Their convictions reveal a deep sense of responsibility, compassion and moral clarity in decision-making.

"It's our duty to pursue our biggest purpose." – Edson.

4. Entrepreneurship and Finance as a Vector for Change

Both men view their ventures not just as economic engines, but as a form of service - a calling. Business and finance are a tool. As Nikolaus explains, tools can be used like a scalpel to heal, a guillotine to harm, or a vegetable peeler for everyday good. Their impact depends entirely on decisions as to its purpose.

Reflections on the Angello Network and it's Values

Nikolaus confesses to being "in the most privileged demographic ever to walk this planet." He explains that his great-great-grandfather was once the most powerful man in Europe. He has two master's degrees from the London School of Economics and Vienna University, respectively. He studied in France and went to school in Switzerland. Yet he is the least qualified academically in his family; he is the only one who doesn't have a doctorate. His wife has two doctorates, his father was a professor, his grandfather was a professor.

"But relatively, from where I'm coming from, I'm the idiot. So really, birth is a lottery, and all of that served me nothing. I had no clue what I wanted to do. I was completely lost." – Nikolaus.

Having drawn this word-picture, Nikolaus goes on to testify to a transformational encounter during a trip to Burkina Faso in the 1990s. Although he describes himself as having been "lost," he had a long-standing sense of justice and an inclination towards Africa. He was struck by the beauty and dignity of the people in Burkina Faso. The church party he was with were giving aid to a local building project in which a handwritten contract had been drawn up in French and signed by the village leader. A year later there was a dispute; the village leader then quoted the relevant passage from the contract in French, a language he didn't speak, and told Nikolaus to look it up in the written contract. The leader had memorized the sounds when the contract was originally read to him, and a year later could quote it verbatim in a language he hardly knew! This was a revelatory moment for Nikolaus:

"I've never seen a similar kind of intellectual feat, and I'm still impressed, and I'm still moved by this." – Nikolaus.

It made Nikolaus realise that birth is a lottery and what really matters are the choices you make and the responsibilities you choose to shoulder.

"Where you're born, how you're born, who you are, is the

lottery ... and then your journey starts." – Nikolaus.
The encounter with the village leader in Burkina Faso reshaped Nikolaus' understanding of dignity, capability and service and taught him that intelligence is not determined by formal education. His mindset shifted from delivering solutions to listening, learning, and co-building with local partners.

"It's not your gifts you're proud of. It's your choices. Who you choose to become." – Nikolaus.

In stark contrast to Nikolaus' family background, Edson's grandfather was the first person in the family to be educated, and he ensured his children and grandchild received the same privilege. Edson witnessed how education empowered his parents and his uncles, enabling them to become leaders in their community. Edson's grandfather was a role model for him, and taught him the value of both education and faith.

"But then I've also seen the power of education. I've seen the power of one individual, in this case, my grandfather, having purpose and having faith, a very religious man, and what that did in actually transforming our family. And I think that is where my inspiration began, because I have seen ... my uncles come from this very small village and transform communities in different ways." – Edson.

Although Nikolaus comes from privilege and Edson from poverty, both men had a keen sense of justice from an early age.

"And for me, it's all started with this one individual who is my role model. And then going through school, I had been very, very curious and also passionate. I think I had a strong sense of what I call justice." – Edson.

"And I had the fortune and the privilege to join a church trip of my community to Burkina Faso ... the pastor would just take young people, 20 of them, and go to Burkina Faso. This is the early 90s, and I was always very interested, and also the

sense of justice was very prevalent. And this is the only thing that I had in terms of a vision." – Nikolaus.

Both men identify fully with the value of social justice, and their lives and their work reflect the values and vision of the Angello network. Their reflections affirm that the spirit of Angello — purpose-rooted collaboration and empowerment across borders — is being lived out in their partnership and work. Angello creates space for authentic voices from across the globe to be heard, especially those from emerging markets. In amplifying these stories, the network promotes unity across diverse cultures, showcasing the richness that emerges when life, work and faith are integrated. Nikolaus and Edson's relationship, which is a cross-continental, cross-generational partnership, embodies this spirit of unity in diversity. It reflects Angello's mission to build bridges and nurture shared purpose among leaders from different walks of life.

The Angello platform highlights voices often overlooked in global conversations. For Edson, this is particularly meaningful as it aligns with his commitment to creating visibility and opportunities for entrepreneurs in Uganda and beyond. The shared belief of both men is that wisdom, innovation and leadership are not the preserve of the economically privileged. On the contrary, they thrive in the margins where purpose, resilience and creativity meet.

A central value of Angello is encouraging purpose-driven leadership in business—leaders who draw from spiritual conviction to guide their decisions, steward resources and serve others. Nikolaus and Edson model this through ventures that prioritize dignity, sustainability and justice above profit.

The Angello network's commitment to transforming conversations into published case studies and learning tools mirrors Relevant Ventures' own desire to document, share and scale what works. Both view storytelling as a powerful form of influence that can inspire others to move on the same path.

The spirit of the early Church as captured in Acts 2: 42–47 is clearly woven into the fabric of Nikolaus and Edson's work. Their stories reflect a living expression of shared purpose, generosity, fellowship and transformative service deeply aligned with the values at the heart of the Angello network. At the core of Relevant Ventures and the Purpose Pool is a belief in collaboration, not control. Success is not measured by individual gain, but by collective progress. Their work demonstrates that sustainable ventures emerge when ownership is shared and resources are mobilized for the common good.

"Our contribution is to see, to do and to inspire." – Edson.

Both Nikolaus and Edson operate on the principle that true partnership is built on mutual respect and dignity, not hierarchy. Their approach is marked by openness and vulnerability, sharing not only their successes but also their personal histories, doubts and formative experiences. This authenticity builds trust and creates space for honest dialogue, learning and growth across cultural and generational lines. Instead of imposing solutions, Nikolaus and Edson focus on enabling others, particularly local entrepreneurs, to realize their own visions. They are relational and empowering, helping others develop the tools, confidence and capacity to lead change in their communities.

"I see us at Relevant as enablers." – Edson.

Underlying their business philosophy is a belief that entrepreneurship can be a form of transformative ministry, a vehicle to serve others and glorify life. Whether through investing in small-scale businesses or designing inclusive financing models, their work is rooted in a desire to empower communities to transform and to thrive.

In all these ways, Nikolaus and Edson embody the values of a modern-day Acts Community, one committed to authenticity, generosity, fellowship and transformation through service.

Future Vision

Looking ahead, Nikolaus and Edson are united by a bold ambition to scale what is working and to contribute meaningfully to a global shift toward a purpose-driven economy. A central question shapes their forward trajectory: "*How can we scale what is working?*"

Relevant Ventures is actively working to systematize its venture-building approach, refining the tools and methodologies that have enabled early success. By codifying what works, they hope to support more entrepreneurs, especially in underserved regions, with frameworks that are adaptable, inclusive, and effective.

A critical part of this vision is bridging the financing gap for early-stage social enterprises. Edson, drawing from his own journey and work with the Purpose Pool, is focused on ensuring that small, promising ventures can access the resources they need to grow, especially in the "*missing middle*" where capital is often scarce.

Their goal is not only to fund impactful enterprises but to demonstrate that purpose-driven businesses can also be financially viable, thereby attracting more capital to these spaces and changing the narrative around investing in marginalised markets. At the heart of their work lies a long-term mission to help birth what Nikolaus calls a "purpose economy," an economy where business and finance are re-purposed to serve people, planet and spiritual flourishing.

"We don't live in that work world yet ... but that's our mission, to accelerate the shift to this purpose-driven economy, not by necessarily writing about it or lamenting about it or activism, but through entrepreneurship, through building viable businesses that work under these kinds of visions." – Nikolaus.

The way ahead is not abstract. It's grounded in practical, tested models that combine spiritual conviction, economic creativity and community collaboration. For Nikolaus and Edson, building the future means building now — on purpose, with purpose.

Closing Reflections on the Conversation

This conversation with Nikolaus Hutter and Edson Niwamanya offers more than a story of collaboration; it is a powerful call to purpose. Through shared conviction, deep mutual trust and spiritual alignment, their friendship has become a beacon for others seeking to lead businesses that are not only economically sustainable, but also socially impactful and spiritually grounded. Their words capture the heart of their mission:

"As humans, we are all good. We're all pursuing something better and bigger than ourselves. And I think it's all about starting where you are through your story, with your individual story, with your individual purpose, and ... challenging yourself to make a contribution. It could be through a community group. It could be through a visit to Uganda, it could be through anything, and it's our duty to pursue our biggest purpose." – Edson.

"It's not your gifts you're proud of. It's your choices, who you choose to become and what choices you make to try to be the best version of yourself." – Nikolaus.

Together, Edson and Nikolaus embody what it means to live and lead with intention, fusing purpose, work and impact in ways that uplift others and challenge prevailing norms. Their journey is an invitation to all. Whether you're an entrepreneur, investor, or purpose-seeker, begin where you are, with what you have, and with who you are. Let their example serve as a reminder that when love informs action and purpose shapes enterprise, transformation is not only possible ... it's inevitable.

Integrity with Derek Kessen and Anatol Malancea

Introduction

Derek Kessen is the Managing Partner of Heron Group, a management consulting and investment management firm based in Chicago with additional offices in Nairobi, Kenya. With a client and investment portfolio spanning over 40 countries across Africa, Asia and the Americas, Derek is passionate about the transformative role business can play in delivering economic and social outcomes in both developed and developing communities.

Anatol Malancea is a visionary entrepreneur and impact-driven business leader, the co-founder and CEO of Uniqa Wall Systems, a ground-breaking modular housing company in Moldova that produces energy-efficient, factory-made homes for the European market. In addition to his entrepreneurial pursuits, Anatol chairs an NGO called Communitas, which supports young entrepreneurs, vulnerable children, and communities in Moldova. He has also been active in facilitating relief efforts to Ukrainian refugees, demonstrating his commitment to social impact beyond business. With frequent travel between Europe and the U.S., Anatol is passionate about transformational investing, ecosystem building, and fostering sustainable economic development in Moldova and beyond. His leadership and dedication to both business and social causes position him as a key player in entrepreneurship and social impact.

Derek and Anatol, members of the Angello network, share their entrepreneurial journeys, leadership philosophies and faith-driven business practices in this interview. Both men bring unique perspectives on how biblical principles shape business operations, relationships and impact. Their conversation delves into the intersection of faith and business, offering valuable insights for fellow entrepreneurs building purpose-driven enterprises with social impact. Through their experiences, they illustrate how business can be a vehicle for success and a platform for meaningful transformation of communities. (*See the bios of Derek and Anatol in Appendix One*).

This interview reveals how deeply Derek and Anatol are committed to creating meaningful social impact. Derek recalls his concern at not being able to contact Anatol's Moldova factory to find out if they were safe during the early stages of the conflict in Ukraine, and that was because Anatol had closed the factory to send his entire team to the border. There, they delivered approximately 800 meals a day and covered the cost of paid fuel for the refugees to be driven to wherever they had contacts.

Leadership and Impact

Derek grew up in a farming community in the Midwest. From a young age he learned by watching his parents that many Americans leave their investment portfolio decisions to investment advisors they don't really know that well, and he became determined to learn about finance and economics. Derek describes himself as a *"financial plumber … the guy who knows how all the things underneath work,"* having run the analytics desk at Performance Trust Capital Partners in Chicago, working with community banks across the United States and beyond. Derek met Anatol when he was transitioning towards founding what has now become the Heron Group, which manages a venture debt fund as well and an equity fund that invests in growth-stage companies, and is preparing to launch a third fund, all three of which are geared for emerging markets. Derek regards this transition as a calling from God.

"God was making it very clear to me that he was pulling me to something different, and he was asking me to use my gifts

in a different way. " – Derek

Anatol's Uniqa Wall Systems company exports modular homes to Western Europe, the Netherlands, and local and neighbouring markets such as Romania and Ukraine. Anatol started the business nine years ago, after working nearly 14 years for a corporate in a select niche of high-end architecture and lighting. Like Derek, he feels he was called to the work he is now doing.

"I was very comfortable. I enjoyed every single day of that work. I travelled the world, I attended the best shows, and we did projects from Saudi Arabia to the UK and the US. And I was really enjoying the ride ... heading toward the golden cage, so to speak, and I realized my calling is not to build a career in the corporate world." – Anatol.

Initially, he was uncertain as to what God was calling him to, but it soon became clear that he should commit to Moldova and that his work was "not a job to be done alone." Following the break-up of the Soviet Union Moldova had been through several economic crises, including hyperinflation and a *"brain drain"* of 30% of the population with the subsequent disintegration of families. Corruption was rife, and the country was in a state of decay. That stark reality compared to the luxurious world of famous architects and world-renowned trade shows, led Anatol to feel he should be contributing towards transforming the situation in Moldova.

Having befriended some businessmen from the Netherlands for whom he was consulting 'pro bono', one of them felt strongly motivated to invest in Anatol's idea to make prefabricated homes using a patented technology from the Netherlands. In that way, jobs could be created that would keep young fathers at home, stimulating the local economy, rather than looking for jobs abroad that would separate them from their families. The demand from the Netherlands grew quickly, including projects for the Dutch government for which they produced a bespoke design with multiple cost-efficient and aesthetic solutions. The necessity for further capital to scale the venture led Anatol to explore the environment of purpose-driven impact investing, including the Angello network at the time Derek was in transition and becoming attracted to the values of the network. For both men, the environment seemed "*too good to be true*," even more so for Derek when he learnt more about Anatol and Uniqa, and the growing values-driven entrepreneurial businesses in Moldova:

"So hearing of this profitable business that built a product that was good for the environment, that created jobs in the short term, but was part of reclaiming good jobs for a whole nation, that was keeping families together, and that was a picture in a part of their community where entrepreneurs were getting together, not just the leaders of Uniqa, but the leaders of other businesses, were getting together and thinking about their community and their country more broadly, and saying, How can our businesses play a role in the future of our nation. I mean, that was crazy." – Derek

Anatol realized that not only did he need the finance to take advantage of his company's momentum, he also needed the expertise of an investor would be prepared not only to provide capital, but who would also act as a sounding board and offer his knowledge of Western systems of business and finance, so that Uniqa could become *"a bridge for entrepreneurs in Moldova."* Anatol's visionary leadership extended far beyond the interests of his own company, and in Derek he had discovered the perfect, values-aligned partner.

Derek describes how he and Anatol were re-introduced through a mutual friend and after that, things moved quickly.

"And as we dug in, we started realizing they had about four years worth of orders that if they just had enough capacity, they would be able to fulfil those orders. And lo and behold, on the same property adjacent to where they're currently located, there was an abandoned factory that just needed some work to be retrofitted to expand their capacity. Also,

an investment would help them hire a few more people and catch up on some of those orders. So that felt 'Wow!' ... This is all making a lot of sense. – Derek.

The war in Ukraine broke out at the time Derek's team was in the final stages of due diligence, and top of his mind was "how to balance and think about risk and reward at the same time." When he and his partners discovered Anatol had closed his factory to rush his team to the border on behalf of the refugees, their response was unequivocal:

"How can we not get involved in a business that is willing to love their neighbour like that at short term personal sacrifice? ... There's a lot of businesses that don't make it. 8 out of 10 fail. If we lose one because of this situation, then we can live with that, because we want to come alongside the people who were meeting the needs of their neighbour in such a material way at great personal cost." – Derek.

Nevertheless, Anatol regards the decision made by Derek and his partners to invest as very brave. Anatol and his friends were the first generation of entrepreneurs in the Soviet Union. Venturing into business was frowned upon by both government and the church, and they were viewed as entering a corrupt world contrary to their faith and everything they were used to. For these reasons, explains Anatol, they endeavoured from the very beginning to be an example of integrity, creating meaningful jobs for people to return to Moldovia and be united with their families and a working environment in which they were treated with dignity, respect, with regular salaries from which taxes paid in full, "*nothing under the table.*"

Anatol played a personal role in co-ordinating this. He ensured his company was an example for other businesses, helping to grow a community of like-minded entrepreneurs. As a result of paying taxes in full without delays over a several years, Anatol's company was awarded a diploma by the government,

"I think it's probably for the first time when we see that even

the government appreciates business with integrity." – Anatol.

Anatol's social commitment never wavers. Having helped thousands of refugees from Ukraine cross the border, they have established a Food Bank at the Uniqa factory, to which their clients from Germany and Netherlands ship truckloads of food and clothing and whatever is needed. At any given point in time, there were 1000s of Ukrainian refugees in the vicinity of the factory and they have been able to help with that through their partnership with a Deloitte company out of Germany by erecting houses for families without charge.

"That's really a phenomenal life-transforming project, not only in the lives of the beneficiaries who are receiving a home in literally three days, but also (has) a transformative impact in the lives of the participants ...Often consultants in the corporate world have never been, and sometimes they've never heard of, countries like Moldova. We provide them a very powerful experience in an emerging market where not only are they part of an experience where, well, miraculously, in three days, a house is given to a family, but they experience a culture, a new country that is struggling from Communism to free market but also seeing some social needs. And their lives are, I think, equally impacted by the experience." – Anatol.

Both Derek and Anatol build their leadership on biblical principles, and their businesses reflect their values. They emphasise the importance of investing in people rather than focusing solely on profits, believing that businesses thrive when they prioritise well-being of employees and communities. Mentorship is also a central aspect of their leadership as they actively share their knowledge and experiences to equip the next generation of faith-driven business leaders.

Beyond mentorship, they leverage their business influence to drive social change by using their resources and opportunities to address pressing societal needs. Their involvement in the Angello network further strengthens a community of entrepreneurs who integrate faith and ethical business practices into their work. Through their leadership, they model a values-based approach that inspires others to build businesses rooted in integrity and service.

As Derek and Anatol illustrate, leadership is not defined by authority but by the ability to inspire, serve, and create opportunities for others. Having responded to God's call, they exemplify the words of Micah Ch. 6: 8:

"He has shown you, O mortal, what is good. And what does the Lord require of you? To act justly, and to love mercy, and to walk humbly with your God."

Challenges and Lessons

Both Derek and Anatol made deliberate choices to move from secure careers to engage in 'working for good.' They encountered significant challenges, not the least of which were the residual complexities presented by the collapse of the Soviet Union; these present numerous obstacles to entrepreneurs in the former Soviet satellites who are seeking integration into capital markets. The COVID-19 pandemic and the war in Ukraine added further challenges for Anatol and Derek, testing their resilience, their willingness to take righteous risks, and their ability to adapt. In difficult circumstances, Derek and Anatol have navigated ethical dilemmas by ensuring that their businesses remain aligned with their faith-driven values. Even though they were raised in radically different cultures, their successes can be directly attributed to the common denominator of their Christian faith.

The opportunity of mentorship as an intern in a "*phenomenal*" company in the US proved to be a platform where Anatol "*learned a lot of great things ... not only how to lead, but also how to start and expand businesses.*" Anatol's description of how he and Derek became partners and established a friendship shows that he is very relational. Businesses can't rise alone - collaboration is crucial. It was through a network of contacts and friends, including the Angello network, that their partnership came about at a time just right to acquire the property which became the factory for his modular housing business.

"Miraculously, I think, we kept bumping into each other ... a lot of friends and common contacts spoke highly of Derek, and we ended up talking about investment in our company, which came at a very crucial time, right in the time when COVID and the war in Ukraine started, which helped us buy an expansion of our property ... since then, we are strong as friends, also participating at events beyond our business, in that space of impact." – Anatol.

Derek relates that his determination from an early age to learn about finance was born out of a concern that people were too trustful of their financial advisors. His business calls for balancing the risk and reward connected with ventures in emerging markets where many unpredictable factors are at play; this requires a discerning ability to trust not only the people leading such ventures, but also other potential investment partners. So, from the beginning, Derek deliberately looked for investment partners who were investing in emerging markets *"with a faith-driven lens."*

"And when I say faith driven ... it doesn't necessarily mean that we're only investing in Christians. A lot of the people we invest in do share the same faith as us, but we look for businesses that are really focused on love of their neighbour, and we look for communities of entrepreneurs that do share our Christian faith, that are saying, 'How can we shape our nation?' 'How can we shape our culture through the Gospel?' ... And of course, we're not the ones determining what that impact is supposed to be, or what those things are that are shaping that nation. We're coming alongside that group with the part that we know how to do. We're grabbing a wrench and working on plumbing from a financial standpoint." - Derek.

One of the greatest challenges Derek and Anatol have faced

is managing the tension between business demands and personal faith commitments. Balancing financial sustainability with social responsibility requires careful decision-making, particularly when short-term financial gains conflict with long-term ethical considerations. Further, finding the people who align with the principles of faith-driven entrepreneurship has been crucial in building teams that share their vision and values.

"I met Anatol in this moment where clusters of faith-focused entrepreneurs were really coming together, especially in emerging markets, and they were saying, 'I have an idea of where I want our country, our country's culture, to be shaped and grown, and what kind of businesses work here, but we do still need capital. And so could you come alongside us and be the kind of capital that we're looking for, and how do we learn what that is together? What kind of structure makes the most sense?'" – Derek.

Through their experiences, Derek and Anatol have learned valuable lessons that continue to shape their leadership. They emphasise that consistency in values leads to long-term credibility - maintaining integrity in all business dealings builds trust and lasting relationships. They stress that true success is not measured by financial profit but by the positive impact a business has on its employees, customers, and the broader community. Their challenges have reinforced the importance of obedience to God's calling, even when the path forward is uncertain.

Over the years, nearly 140 Deloitte consultants have come to Moldova through our partnership with Build&Grow — an initiative started by a senior Deloitte consultant to combine team-building with purpose by constructing homes for families in need. These builds are only possible thanks to Uniqa's prefabricated Lego-type wall system and our experienced local team, which allow a full house to be raised in just three days. Some of the Deloitte volunteers have returned four or five times, and many are eager to come again. I believe our company has become a small but meaningful instrument for changing lives.

"We want to show that it's possible to build with honesty, to create impact beyond profit, and to inspire a new generation of entrepreneurs in Moldova." - Anatol

Both men stress the need for work-life balance and a healthy theology of work, recognising that faith and business are not separate spheres but deeply intertwined. What does a healthy "theology of work" look like? Both men refer to the following as lessons learnt, although they humbly admit to shortcomings:

1. Do not allow your work to become your identity.

"I thought that I had a pretty good relationship with work. I thought I was well adjusted. And it wasn't until it wasn't a part of my life anymore that I realized how much it mattered to me ... working through that I had to get to a point where I could look up at God and say, 'It's okay if I never work in finance again.' That was an identity issue and an idol issue within me that had to be dealt with before I could move on into the next season'" – Derek.

2. Make time for God to remain in right relationship with God.

"God doesn't lead you towards redemptive things that you can only achieve if you live un-redemptively to get there ... These are things we're learning, but it really hasn't permeated the workplace yet. What does a healthy Sabbath and balance of life look like when you're around other high achievers? I think it's easy to give each other permission to violate those things. That is a sin. We've been sinning in our work life, even though we've been pursuing a redemptive end." – Derek.

3. Make time for rest, recreation, family and friends.

"I fully resonate with work and life balance, and I think there is

a risk to be driven by results at the expense of rest and often overworking. So that's room for repentance, right there." – Anatol.

4. Although difficult seasons can be transformative and create unseen opportunities that build teamwork, character and faith, it doesn't follow that suffering is an inevitable part of working for the kingdom.

"Our team had a really poor theology … like if it's something we're doing in service of the kingdom, it has to be painful for us. I don't really know how we got there, because I don't believe that when you're doing something that's in alignment with God's purposes … that it always is going to feel good, or that it's always going to feel bad. Neither one of those things necessarily tell you … whether you're on the right path." – Derek.

5. Don't miss out on the joy.

"The reality is, God wants us to have joy. One of the things we're really focused on this year is reclaiming our sense of adventure and community and hospitality and the way that we get to spend time with all the entrepreneurs that are in our portfolio, even the ones we haven't even met yet, because that's an area I think that we've really lost track of." – Derek.

6. Apply discernment to remain obedient to your calling.

"The greatest lesson for me is obedience while discerning God's leading and guidance. I see opportunities that can be very distracting, and I think discerning and being where I'm really led is where I need to focus." - Anatol.

Key Themes and Insights

Faith as a Guide for Business: Derek and Anatol emphasise that faith is not a separate aspect of their professional lives but rather the guiding force behind their business decisions and leadership. Their commitment to faith shapes how they approach challenges, make decisions, and lead others.

"This is the life of an entrepreneur. Challenges are part of the recipe ... are part of a lifestyle... When we are set to do everything with integrity, things beyond our control are in God's control." – Anatol.

The Power of Relationships and Community: Both men highlight the role of genuine relationships in fostering business growth and resilience. Being part of a community like Angello offers both spiritual support and business mentorship. Their professional connection, which started as a meeting in Colorado, turned into a partnership that played a crucial role in supporting Anatol's business through a difficult season.

"… and the encouragement I find is really in this local and global community. So, I'm just very grateful for that." – Anatol.

Learn the Discipline of Discernment: Anatol stresses the importance of discerning God's leading and guidance. Success may bring tempting opportunities that can lead you away from your calling.

"I am not only a Moldovan citizen - I have the full right to live anywhere in Europe or even in the US. It comes with a price to listen, discern and choose to stay obedient to the calling. But it's very rewarding." – Anatol.

Integrity and Ethical Leadership: Derek and Anatol stress that a values-driven approach to business builds long-term success. Ethical decisions, even when difficult, reinforce trust and credibility. Their journeys show that leading with honesty and transparency strengthens businesses and communities alike.

Balancing Profit and Purpose: Both entrepreneurs emphasise that profitability is important, but it should not come at the expense of ethical considerations or social impact.

Their businesses prioritise both financial sustainability and meaningful impact, proving that faith-driven enterprises can thrive while uplifting others.

"But I learned to rejoice, and I do rejoice in that sense of being not only called … but what that obedience could bring, what kind of fruit it can bear, not for me personally, but really for helping lives to be transformed." – Anatol.

Key Principles for Faith-Driven Entrepreneurs

1. Stewardship Over Ownership

Viewing business as a God-given responsibility rather than personal ownership shifts decision-making towards sustainability and impact. Derek and Anatol emphasise that businesses should focus on loving their neighbours and shaping their nations through the Gospel. Their work reflects a deep commitment to using business as a tool for positive transformation rather than just personal gain.

"We look for communities of entrepreneurs who share our Christian faith and are saying, 'How can we shape our nation? How can we shape our culture through the Gospel?'" – Derek.

"How can we not get involved in a business that is willing to love their neighbour like that…" – Derek.

2. Service-Oriented Leadership

Leading with humility and a desire to serve employees, customers and the wider community creates a culture of mutual growth. Anatol's business strives to be an example of integrity, creating meaningful jobs and treating employees with dignity and respect. By fostering a workplace rooted in care and ethical responsibility, he ensures that business success translates into broader societal impact.

"We strive to be an example of integrity, but also to create meaningful jobs for people." – Anatol.

3. Trusting in God's Timing

Success in business requires patience and faith, acknowledging that not all plans unfold as expected, but divine timing is always at play. Anatol's journey, particularly the support he received from Derek during critical moments like the COVID-19 pandemic and the war in Ukraine, illustrates the importance of trusting in God's provision. Their story highlights how unexpected connections and opportunities arise when entrepreneurs stay faithful to their calling.

4. Honesty in Business Dealings

Transparent and ethical business practices ensure credibility and long-term partnerships. Derek and Anatol's approach to business underscores that integrity should never be compromised for short-term gains. They believe that building businesses rooted in honesty not only strengthens relationships but also contributes to long-term stability and influence in the marketplace.

"They're treated with dignity, respect, also salaries and taxes being paid in full, nothing under the table." – Anatol.

5. Creating a Meaningful Work Environment Strengthens Communities

One of the most significant impacts of faith-driven entrepreneurship is job creation that keeps families together and supports the local economy. Anatol and Derek recognise the importance of building businesses that do more than generate profit, providing opportunities that allow individuals to thrive in their own communities rather than seeking work abroad. This principle reinforces the idea that business can be a force for economic stability and family cohesion.

"We strive ... to create meaningful jobs for people who return from other countries and be united and families and to give them a meaningful working environment." – Anatol.

Reflections on the Angello Network and the Acts Community Values

Angello's mission to bridge the gap between faith and business resonates with both leaders, who see it as a powerful space for fostering ethical entrepreneurship, strengthening community ties, and proving that faith-driven businesses can be both profitable and impactful.

The Angello network fosters a strong sense of community among faith-driven entrepreneurs, providing support, accountability, and friendship. It emphasises values such as integrity, love of neighbour, and the importance of creating meaningful impact through business. Being part of this network contributed to bringing Derek and Anatol together in partnership, and being part of this network has reinforced their commitment to using their businesses as vehicles for positive change.

At the heart of Angello's philosophy is its commitment to the Acts Community values of authentic fellowship, discipleship, joy, generosity, service and impact. These principles resonate throughout the stories Derek and Anatol have related in this interview, and they have shaped the way both men approach business and leadership. The principles are not abstract ideals; they are actively lived out in their work, relationships and leadership styles. Derek and Anatol have built, and benefited from, strong, faith-rooted relationships both within the Angello network and in their local contexts. They prioritize relational trust and mutual encouragement, seeing their partners not as colleagues but as brothers and sisters on a shared mission.
Their leadership reflects a discipleship mindset, committed not only to business excellence but also to spiritual formation. Derek adds that friendship removes power dynamics and allows truth-telling.

"We're friends … and I think that the greatest part of whatever this style of entrepreneur and investor relationship is, I can look at our portfolio leaders and say, we're friends … we're in

this together. We are shoulder to shoulder." – Derek.

Derek and Anatol see business as a context for growing in Christ, mentoring others and modelling Kingdom values through daily decisions. For them, leadership is about shaping others through example, integrity and intentional growth. Both leaders carry a contagious sense of joy in their work. Whether navigating challenges or celebrating wins, they approach their roles with hope and gratitude, believing that joy is not dependent on circumstances but rooted in the purpose God has given them. This joy permeates their teams and sets the tone for redemptive workplace culture.

Derek and Anatol practice generosity in how they give their time, share resources, and invest in others. Whether through mentorship, partnership or community engagement, they embody a giving spirit that reflects the early Church's ethic of sharing all things in common for the good of others.

Service is a defining feature of their leadership. They don't lead from a place of authority, but from a desire to serve — lifting others up, empowering local talent and putting the needs of employees, communities and partners ahead of personal gain. This servant-hearted approach builds trust and strengthens the ecosystem around them.

Above all, both men are committed to meaningful, measurable impact. They view business as a vehicle for transformation, creating jobs, restoring dignity and advancing the common good in ways that reflect God's redemptive plan.

Together, Derek and Anatol embody the values of the Acts Community, showing that when business is built on fellowship, discipleship, joy, generosity, service and positive impact, it becomes a powerful expression of faith in action.

Future Vision

Derek and Anatol envision continued growth and impact

through their businesses which are driven by their faith and commitment to their communities. Uniqa is *"in the middle of a large development, nearly 100 homes,"* and expanding land with new investors. Heron is preparing to launch its third emerging markets fund. Looking ahead, both Derek and Anatol are focused on expanding mentorship programmes within the Angello network, developing more business models that integrate faith-based principles, and strengthening global collaborations among faith-driven entrepreneurs. They are dedicated to equipping the next generation with practical business and leadership skills grounded in Christian values.

Closing Reflections

Derek Kessen and Anatol Malancea illuminate the powerful intersection of faith and business. Their stories offer valuable insights and inspiration for fellow entrepreneurs, underscoring the importance of integrity, community and obedience to God's calling. Their careers demonstrate that faith-driven principles can profoundly shape business operations and relationships. This conversation testifies to the transformative power of business where Godly principles are embedded in every decision.

Transformation with Ruben Marian and Daniel Lar

Introduction

Ruben Marian is a Christ-centred entrepreneur from Cluj-Napoca, Romania, dedicated to driving transformation through business and leadership. Ruben and his wife Oana founded UTILBEN, a leading provider of heavy machinery, and have since expanded their investments into agriculture, dermato-cosmetics, and tourism. *(See Ruben's bio in Appendix One)*

Daniel Lar is an investor, a seasoned portfolio manager at Total Specific Solutions, a division of Constellation Software, with extensive experience in managing and growing diverse portfolios. Daniel also serves as a pastor at Teofania Church. *(See Daniel's bio in Appendix One)*

In this conversation Ruben and Daniel give a fascinating account of the growth and work of Guild, an organisation they co-founded to foster entrepreneurial systems and community development while equipping entrepreneurs for urban mission and discipleship. The mission training is provided by the Timothy Urban Mission Training Program, which was initiated by Daniel. Both men actively support the Angello Network, embodying the conviction that faith and business are inseparable. Their entrepreneurial efforts flow from a higher calling to build communities, transform lives, and demonstrate that business can serve as a platform for mission.

Leadership and Impact

Ruben Marian and Daniel Lar are passionate about the power of personal spiritual transformation to bring kingdom values into the business world and transform nations. This conviction grew after they founded Guild, a concept based on the mediaeval guilds which served as learning and support communities for practitioners in different trades.

Daniel explains that the purpose of GUILD is to invest in businesses and guide their leaders in understanding what it takes to be "a great executive, entrepreneur, manager, or professional" while making a positive impact on their country. Those who are open to it are encouraged to explore spiritual meaning in environments "where they can experience more about God and grow as disciples." This emphasis on discipleship, rather than solely on business ethics, is what sets GUILD apart from other Christian business networks. Its volunteer-driven structure, focus on organic growth, and vision to serve as a replicable model further distinguish it. The Timothy Urban Mission Training Program exemplifies this approach, providing participants with an environment to deepen their understanding of Scripture and discover their unique calling as they serve God in their communities.

Daniel describes Guild as an "outreach into society," in which Daniel and Ruben feel called to be present as 'salt and light'. He explains that before Guild came into being, both men had been involved in events that depended upon Western speakers. Frustrated by the amount of work that went into these "one-time'" events, they saw the need for an organic, locally led, Romanian-based network that could grow together as a community. Daniel explains that Guild started out of a need for like-minded leaders to inspire one another. They were surprised at how quickly it grew into a national movement – they did not realise how great the need was.

"We started one group with three friends inviting their other three friends … But we did not imagine that this will grow to so many cities in Romania now, and we will have so many groups." – Daniel.

Guild currently has 25 groups in 7 cities in Romania. Both men see this growth as God's work, with unlimited potential.

" ... this is part of what God is doing. Now we see the potential of this being a foundation for community-building and for a real network of leaders that can really bring transformation in their city and then in the nation." – Ruben.

Ruben tells of how lives are being transformed within the Guild communities. People who were successful in business but did not have the joy only Jesus can provide, have experienced spiritual transformation, together with their families. Now these same people are making other disciples in the marketplace. Guild offers a creative, positive vision for the future.

"So it's a unique opportunity, I think, where people in society are very open for God. They've tried different ways to be happy and to achieve what the world can offer, but really they are looking for other solutions that can make them happy and joyful long term. So we offer community ... and in this community they experience kingdom values, generosity, collaboration, and this transforms their hearts and their life, and then they want to contribute. So it's really encouraging."
- Ruben

Daniel explains that the Timothy Urban Mission Program came about when they realised it is just as important to prepare people for mission work in their hometown as it is when sending missionaries to distant lands. It began after leaders in Guild groups started to request materials and tools to support their evangelical endeavours.

"When it's about doing urban missions in our hometown, we don't expect to have to learn something about it. We think we know it, and quite shockingly, very, very often we see people who have, you know, different values, different worldviews from us ... even though most assume that they are Christians, actually many of them are not." – Daniel.

Furthermore, although Daniel and Ruben initially dreamt that Guild could be "a movement among multiple professions in multiple cities," they did not dream it would become international.

"And now it's really humbling to see people from other nations asking us, how can we implement something similar in our nation? And again, we're a movement of volunteers, basically. Now we do have a structure, we do have support system, a staff and so forth, but it's primarily about helping leaders be activated." – Daniel.

Although Ruben humbly states, *"We don't want to be impactful. We only want to be faithful, and we see bigger results for the kingdom,"* his work for the kingdom has had considerable impact both locally and internationally. When Malcolm Johnston asked him to host a FORGE conference in Cluj he took it very seriously because he saw it as an opportunity to bring Romanian business leaders together.

"So I already saw the opportunity for Romanian support, because I was not inviting them to our community or our event. Hey, this was FORGE! That was international, 40 nations coming together, and then I saw this opportunity, so I directly invited leaders. So I was like a catalyst and the facilitator." – Ruben.

Also, having experienced the FORGE conference in Kenya and Egypt, Ruben saw it as an opportunity to "*shape*" the conference to their own Romanian context and give "a voice" to emerging market business leaders, even though this meant having to stand his ground with the organizing partners. The conference proved to be truly advantageous for the growth of entrepreneurial ecosystem in Romania; the leaders from different Romanian organizations, initiatives and movements who attended the conference now meet monthly.

Ruben clarifies his comment about not wanting to be impactful by confessing that when he and Daniel started Guild, he was focused on "being successful in business and having a great impact in the world." But as Guild grew into different cities, he "*saw God at work*" and lives being transformed.

"Experiencing the transformation in people lives was bigger than any business achievement." – Ruben.

Thereafter, he was passionate to see Guild grow as a ministry across all the cities in Romania. It required a lot of effort, but then God led them both into working and learning with the Angello network and the FORGE Movement. On this journey he is learning to 'let go and let God.'

"And I think God is working on my heart to Yeah, to let go of wanting to be successful and to look for impact, but to remain faithful, to love people and to be patient, even in Guild ... I learned that we need to wait for the Lord to see where He's working, and to wait for the invitation to be part of what God is working already, and to listen to the Holy Spirit. And now I can see amazing things that happened in Romania and other nations, and with very, very much less effort compared to some years ago." – Ruben.

Challenges and Lessons

When Ruben and Daniel started Guild, their mission was to invest in businesses and bring business leaders to know Jesus and lead transformed lives. They were surprised to find that while some friends from other churches joined the Guild groups, they did not invite others to join them. It became clear to Ruben and Daniel that although these leaders were attending church, the transformation journey is different for everyone, so it became necessary to differentiate within the groups. Those who "really knew" Jesus, were encouraged and helped to become "ambassadors of Christ in the marketplace and love the city, love the people, and get into the mission, part of the movement." Others were first helped "to encounter Jesus, to meet the Father's love and to receive the Holy Spirit, and to have a transformed life." It was necessary to be open and up-front that Guild is a Holy Spirit-led movement. Rather than being a deterrent, this proved attractive to business leaders.

"We're direct in everything we do. We are professionals in business. We are also Christians. We love the Lord, and we see that the authenticity and the fact that we are open with who we are, it's really making a big impact." – Ruben

The fact that Ruben and Daniel communicate with such positive energy and passion hides the many challenges faced in their context of a developing economy and the social, cultural and political complexities peculiar to Romania.

"You know, we grew up in in a communist country, and then people are like, you know, being so defensive and lots of justifications that people don't seek the Lord, people are not open to that … when, actually, in the right context, there are many people who are open to talk and to explore and who are seeking." - Daniel.

"So there's all these lies and issues that we've lived with sometimes, and a lack of empowerment." – Daniel.

Daniel states that Christ-centred professionals and businesspeople are *"very uniquely positioned in the business world to be salt and light there."* He gives the example of his wife, who is a psychiatrist. She had felt called to the mission field, but a mentor persuaded her to finish her studies because psychiatry can be a mission field in itself, where people who are hurting come for help.

"As entrepreneurs, managers, doctors, you know, we can really be of help, because people trust us due to our position, due to our job, even, and in that context, you know, we can be credible, and … use all that God gave us in terms of position, influence, gifts and so forth, to be able to help." – Daniel.

One of the leadership challenges Ruben and Daniel identify is isolation. Ruben observes that leadership can be a lonely space, particularly for Christians.

"Leadership is quite lonely, especially if you're a Christian.

If you're in leadership in a business, you will not get much support, at least in Romania, from local churches or from others to say, 'Hey, you're doing a good job.'" – Ruben.

The great lesson that Ruben and Daniel emphasise throughout this conversation is the power of a personal, spiritual relationship with Jesus, and the purpose this brings to want others to experience the same, thereby growing communities bonded by a spirit of true communion where each supports the other. The ecosystem that develops from such communities provides a supporting structure for continued growth of purpose-driven business enterprises. Faith is both the catalyst and the sustainer.

"Learning really happens, not just by reading, but by being in a community, and also working with people, blessing people, trying to help people, and then eventually, you know, either you do it part of the church team or in a Guild team or in a different context, we want people to continue and be practitioners, because we believe we want to learn from practitioners." – Daniel.

Daniel explains that the Guild project and its offspring the Timothy Program were born out of a need for community, a learning community of practitioners who help each other to become better. Because there was a need for a *"more conversational context ... where people discuss and debate and struggle together with the same major questions,"* the Timothy Program offers a series of meetings to understand the gospel. Daniel describes it as *"bringing the good news in a relational, non-formal context ... a process which is open for people to ask questions."*

"It's about community, about the process, about having the time to ask questions and to debate and having people who mentor you." – Daniel.

Daniel mentions that there were several struggles, and there still are. From experience, they have learnt that in mission work there is a danger of linking identity with the success of missions, and that can be *"really crushing and challenging."* So they spend training time on identity, transformation, restoration and healing as well as understanding that helping people come to Christ does not depend upon intellectual knowledge.

"Of course, we need to start with the Bible and have intellectual answers, but you will not outsmart somebody into the kingdom. Sometimes we think we can outsmart somebody into the kingdom, and it doesn't work that way. I mean, we can love somebody into the kingdom, but we cannot outsmart somebody into the kingdom." – Daniel.

Balancing business responsibilities with personal faith is an ongoing challenge. The pressures of leadership, decision-making and financial management can easily become all-consuming, making it crucial to remain grounded through intentional prayer, accountability and a commitment to biblical wisdom. Seeking counsel from trusted mentors and surrounding oneself with a faith-driven community helps entrepreneurs navigate these pressures with clarity and purpose. Ruben and Daniel have found the interaction and support within the Angello network invaluable and inspirational.

"Sometimes you might feel alone, and there's not too many people doing what you're doing. But then you meet people from other countries who have similar challenges." – Daniel.

During difficult seasons, whether facing economic downturns, business setbacks, or opposition, maintaining faith becomes essential. Trusting in God's provision and guidance requires spiritual resilience, a willingness to surrender control and confidence that God's plans are greater than immediate circumstances. In these moments, faith is not just a personal belief but a practical anchor that provides strength and clarity. Ultimately, every challenge presents an opportunity to grow in trust and dependence on God. Authenticity and transparency are the basic values behind everything Daniel and Ruben do.

Key Themes and Insights

Business as a Calling. For Ruben and Daniel business is not just about making money; it is a calling to serve and honour God. Their approach is centred on trusting God's guidance in decision-making, ensuring that their business operations reflect gospel values. For them, entrepreneurship is inseparable from God's mission.

"We are very uniquely positioned as Christians in the business world to be salt and light there." – Daniel.

"And then you see the process, and you see somebody ... be converted, really understand, and not just understand, believe in God and live with God and experience, you know, the Spirit of God leading them, and then become involved in helping, helping others. It's, such an honour to be part of that." – Daniel.

Integrity and Ethical Leadership. Maintaining integrity in business can be difficult, especially when faced with challenges or opportunities that compromise ethical standards. Both leaders stress the importance of making decisions that align with gospel values. Their commitment to honesty and ethical leadership has allowed them to build businesses that earn trust and respect in their industries.

"We want to use all that God gave us in terms of position, influence, gifts and so forth, to be able to help." – Daniel.

Stewardship and Responsibility. Ruben and Daniel view their businesses as platforms for service rather than personal gain. They see themselves as stewards of God's resources rather than owners, responsible for using resources wisely and ensuring their work benefits others. This mindset influences their approach to financial management, employee relations and business growth, ensuring that their enterprises reflect God's kingdom principles. Their businesses are vehicles for blessing others and advancing kingdom values.

"We believe we want to learn from practitioners. And we want to help people become practitioners in this because otherwise, you know, we can just think and overthink sometimes, and things don't happen because God wants us to obey and to do things." – Daniel.

"We only want to be faithful, and we see bigger results for the kingdom." – Ruben.

Resilience in the Face of Challenges: Running a business comes with inevitable hardships, from financial struggles to external opposition. However, both leaders emphasise that these difficulties are opportunities to trust in God and grow spiritually. Their testimonies highlight how faith provides strength and perseverance in adversity.

"We need to wait for the Lord to see where he's working, and to wait for the invitation to be part of what God is working already, and to listen to the Holy Spirit." – Ruben.

"We can love somebody into the kingdom, but we cannot outsmart somebody into the kingdom." – Daniel.

The Power of Community and Fellowship: Isolation is one of the greatest challenges for entrepreneurs, which is why Ruben and Daniel emphasise the importance of surrounding themselves with like-minded believers. They actively build fellowship, mentorship and partnerships with others who share their values. Guild itself is testimony to the need for fellowship.

"A common mission drives unity in a way that's really special."
- Daniel.

This sense of community fosters collaboration over competition, strengthening businesses and uplifting entire industries. Through their experiences, Ruben and Daniel demonstrate that faith and business are not separate pursuits but are deeply intertwined. Their journey testifies to the power of faith-driven entrepreneurship, encouraging others to lead with integrity, serve with purpose, and trust in God's provision every step of the way.

Key Principles for Faith-Driven Entrepreneurs

1. Faith as the Foundation of Enterprise

Ruben and Daniel's entrepreneurial ventures are founded on faith, demonstrating how biblical principles can shape business operations, leadership and personal growth. For them, business is a calling to serve and glorify God. Every decision, whether big or small, should be guided by faith, trusting in God's provision and direction even in times of uncertainty. They measure success by the positive impact their endeavours have on building and serving ethical business communities throughout the nation and beyond. Faith is not an add-on – it is the core of their entrepreneurial and evangelical efforts. By placing faith at the centre of their business practices, they ensure that their work aligns with a greater purpose, bringing honour to God in all they do.

"If I know God loves me, and I sense God loves me, and I am led by His Spirit, I think we can be the kind of people ... that God can take a risk on and send us somebody that he wants us to help." – Daniel.

2. Integrity and Stewardship

Integrity and stewardship go hand in hand. Integrity is the cornerstone of a business built on biblical principles. Authenticity, transparency and ethical decision-making must be non-negotiable, even when difficult choices arise. Faith-driven entrepreneurs recognise that they are not the owners of their businesses; they are the stewards of the resources entrusted to them. This perspective shifts the focus from personal gain to responsible management, ensuring that finances, time and influence are used wisely to reflect God's glory. By leading with integrity and practising wise stewardship, they create businesses that are not only successful but also sustainable and impactful.

"We are relaxed now ... we don't need to prove anything. We don't want to be impactful. We only want to be faithful." - Ruben.

"We want people to continue and be practitioners ... because otherwise, you know, we can just think and overthink sometimes, and things don't happen because God wants us to obey and to do things." – Daniel.

Ruben and Daniel lead with transparency and a deep sense of responsibility for the resources and the skills entrusted to them.

3. Service-Oriented Leadership

True leadership is not about authority or control; it is about serving others. Entrepreneurs who integrate faith into their business understand that employees, clients and stakeholders should be treated with dignity and respect, recognising their intrinsic value beyond their economic contributions. A service-oriented leader seeks to uplift those around them, creating a culture of trust, collaboration and care. Businesses that prioritise service extend their influence beyond the workplace, actively contributing to the well-being of their communities through acts of generosity, mentorship, and social responsibility. Ruben and Daniel prioritize people over profit, using their organisations to uplift and disciple others.

"The biggest and the best investment we can make is in people's lives." – Daniel.

"The blessing and the joy that I had there, experiencing the transformation in people's lives, was bigger than any business achievement." – Ruben.

4. Resilience and Faith in Challenges

Every business faces challenges, but for faith-driven entrepreneurs these moments become opportunities for growth and spiritual refinement. Difficult times test not only business acumen but also trust in God's plan. Rather than succumbing to fear or discouragement, resilient leaders lean into their faith, believing that trials are a means of strengthening character and deepening dependence on God. Ruben and Daniel see challenges as opportunities for spiritual growth and deeper dependence on God. Endurance is built through adversity, and those who remain steadfast in their faith emerge stronger, with a greater capacity to lead and inspire others. Faith-driven entrepreneurs embrace challenges as part of their spiritual journey. Ruben and Daniel have learned to trust God's timing and provision.

"I learned that we need to wait for the Lord to see where he's working ... and to listen to the Holy Spirit." – Ruben.

"Sometimes we think we can outsmart somebody into the kingdom, and it doesn't work that way." – Daniel.

5. Fellowship and Community

For faith-driven entrepreneurs, surrounding themselves with like-minded believers is essential, not only for accountability but also for encouragement, wisdom, and support during challenging times. Fellowship provides a foundation where values are reinforced, and purpose is clarified.

Guild was born out of the need to combat the isolation that many leaders face and to foster authentic relationships rooted in shared faith. It offers a space where leaders can connect, grow, and support one another in both their professional and spiritual journeys.

Rather than viewing others as competition, Ruben and Daniel champion a culture of collaboration. When businesses work together with a shared mission, they generate greater impact. A strong community of faith-driven leaders nurtures innovation, mutual support, and a legacy of ethical, purpose-driven entrepreneurship.

"In community, we can be creative. We can get vision. And if we walk together, God can give us amazing vision about the future." – Ruben.

"Mature leaders really cooperate in pursuing the same mission." – Daniel.

Reflections on the Angello Network and the Acts Community Values

Ruben Marian and Daniel Lar emphasize the importance of being part of a strong, faith-based network like Angello and FORGE. Business, they believe, is not meant to be done in isolation. Instead, entrepreneurs who seek to honour God through their work should surround themselves with a supportive community that shares their values, encourages accountability, and fosters collaboration.

"In Angello network, I learned about ecosystem. I did not know the term ecosystem that can apply to marketplace ministry, what we were doing in Romania … I understood the role that we had to integrate, to be facilitators in the Romanian ecosystem, to invite people together, to help build bridges in a nation where we did not know how to collaborate." – Ruben.

As Ruben outlines, hosting FORGE in Cluj became a turning point: "We did not take only the role of a host … I said that, hey, we have the opportunity now to help the Romanian ecosystem to come together … I was like a catalyst and the facilitator, and I invited more leaders to the table. And that was such a blessing."

"What happens there is really phenomenal … mature leaders really cooperate in pursuing the same mission … communities of leaders who are really learning communities … that creates

that kind of friendship, of camaraderie, of us doing something together in similar ways, but different in different parts of the world." – Daniel.

Together, Ruben and Daniel see Angello as a vital space for connection, mentorship and shared learning, where values like faith, integrity, and generosity are not just spoken but lived.

"It's a band of brothers. We come together and we share, and we are accountable to each other, and we encourage. It's not easy to be, you know, the only visionary. It's hard. It's very nice to find friends that think alike and come together." – Ruben.

They stress the importance of generosity, sharing knowledge, and creating opportunities for collaboration rather than competition. The mission of Angello aligns seamlessly with their own - building businesses that honour God, create lasting impact, and cultivate a culture of faith-driven entrepreneurship.

Future Vision

Ruben and Daniel envision a future where faith-driven business becomes a movement of collaboration, integrity and excellence in which Christian entrepreneurs transform industries and workplaces into spaces of ministry. For them, business is far more than profit; it is a platform where employees and clients alike can experience God's love through daily interactions.

The key to growing this platform is personal spiritual transformation. Their dream is to see GUILD and the Timothy Training Programme replicated both nationally and internationally. Ruben describes their vision as a future where leaders live out their faith with integrity and courage, making disciples and cultivating a culture of generosity, collaboration, and hope. They believe God is raising a new generation of leaders transformed by Christ, using their influence as instruments of mission and restoration. Together, they aspire to see cities and nations renewed through the power of God's Kingdom. As Daniel shared: *"GUILD is already in seven cities.*

Our dream is to see this in every major city in Romania - and why not beyond?" Reflecting on the Timothy Program, he added: *"It's not just skills. It's healing, identity, restoration. We are equipping a generation to serve with wholeness."*

Looking ahead, they hope to inspire and equip the next generation of faith-driven entrepreneurs to create businesses that are not only successful but are incubators for an environment in which the Holy Spirit is given room to work.
"Imagine workplaces where people encounter God's love through daily interactions. That is the future of faith-driven business." – Ruben.

Closing Reflections on the Conversation

This conversation highlights how Ruben and Daniel's approach to business and leadership development is both spiritual and practical. They call entrepreneurs to embrace business as mission — where faith is the foundation that shapes every decision, from finances to relationships.

"Every decision, from finances to relationships, is part of glorifying God." – Daniel.

Their testimonies reveal that transformation is possible when leaders build with integrity, steward resources responsibly, and foster authentic communities.

"We are not building empires. We are building people. And through people, God is transforming cities." – Ruben.

Faith-driven entrepreneurship, they affirm, is both an inspiration and a challenge. It invites business leaders to ask hard questions: Are their ventures more than profit-generating enterprises? Do they serve as platforms to glorify God and extend God's kingdom?

Beyond personal conviction, they stress the power of

community. A strong network of like-minded believers provides encouragement, accountability, and shared wisdom for navigating the complexities of business. In their words and witness, Ruben and Daniel remain adamant that entrepreneurs who embrace this calling have the potential to reshape industries, uplift communities, and reflect God's kingdom in the marketplace.

"The biggest and the best investment we can make is in people's lives ... it's not my achievement ... it's really miracles I see." – Daniel.

"The blessing and the joy that I had there, experiencing the transformation in people's lives, was bigger than any business achievement." – Ruben.

Ruben and Daniel remind us that faith and business are not separate pursuits but intertwined aspects of a mission-driven life.

"We don't need to prove anything. We don't want to be impactful. We only want to be faithful." – Ruben.

"You want to be part of that ... not that we can do it, but rather that God is doing it." – Daniel.

By leading with integrity, practicing good stewardship, and prioritizing service, they demonstrate that business can be a powerful force for good, transforming not only companies but the lives and communities they touch.

Impact with Smily Rostus

Introduction

Dr. Smily Rostus is the Managing Director of SUREnterprise, leading a diverse portfolio spanning microfinance, livelihood enhancement, veterinary services and information technology. He is on the steering committee of the Angello Network and is a Steward of the FORGE movement. Smily is a visionary entrepreneur and ecosystem builder dedicated to integrating faith with business. Through SUREnterprise, he has helped provide collateral-free loans to vulnerable communities, improving livelihoods in over 300,000 homes. (*See Smily's bio in Appendix One*)

As a member of the Angello network, Smily has contributed to the evolving landscape of Christian entrepreneurship in India, where business is increasingly seen as a means of economic growth and social transformation. Smily shares insights into the shift happening within the entrepreneurial ecosystem, including the rise of business fellowships in churches and the growing collaboration among organisations. He emphasises the integration of Godly principles in business operations, leadership and community building, demonstrating how faith-driven values such as humility, generosity and reconciliation shape both professional and personal relationships. Through his experiences, Smily offers valuable lessons on balancing work and family life while fostering a sustainable and impactful entrepreneurial ecosystem that aligns with God's purpose.

Leadership and Impact

Smily Rostus describes a shift in the entrepreneurship ecosystem in India, where churches are beginning to hold monthly business fellowship meetings, prayer meetings for businesspeople and conferences.

"Christian entrepreneurs are slowly coming out of churches to be able to start businesses."

When Smily was growing up in India, this didn't happen. Now, the ecosystem is evolving, with more and organizations providing programmes for entrepreneurs and funding agencies willing to put impact and investment capital into India. Smily operates from New Delhi, where a local fund is about to be created with Christian entrepreneurs willing to put money at risk to uplift people. Although there are multiple organizations, they don't work together, so Smily is trying to bring collaboration into the ecosystem. Since 2024 they have had some success.

Although Christianity is a minor religion in India, it dates back to the evangelical work of Thomas the Apostle in the first century, so there are pockets of Christianity with deep roots. Also, there are growing numbers of new Christians, particularly in the South. Wherever there is increasing social mobility the concept of starting a business is on the rise. Most young Christians are somewhere on the social mobility ladder and are not tied through necessity to a job or informal trading. Business as a career is gaining social respectability, particularly businesses which have a positive impact in uplifting people in their communities.

Smily and his wife believe their purpose is to bless people through the enterprises they invest in and the work they do, so social impact is high amongst their priorities. Smily is pleased to see that his young daughters recognize this and are already talking about starting their own businesses. Smily is a passionate advocate for enterprises in which faith and business are deeply integrated; he believes true impact comes from building ecosystems that uplift communities. He sees his role a connector, bringing organisations and entrepreneurs together to amplify their collective impact.

"Our primary objective, our goal, is to glorify the Lord, be connected to the Lord. And the secondary objective is to be

connected to people."

His leadership is rooted in kingdom values such as humility, generosity and perseverance, ensuring that his business decisions align with a greater purpose.

Challenges and Lessons

Smily's leadership experiences have taught him to build second-tier leadership within his ventures, ensuring that businesses and initiatives can thrive beyond his direct involvement.

"One of the things that I do is I don't micromanage. Trust people to make good decision and build a team. Delegate. The second level of leadership is very important … where I can rest and say, 'Okay, nothing will happen if I'm not there for a day.'"

He has learnt to prioritise and not spend time on things he does not feel are valuable. Although he will hear out those to whom he has delegated responsibility, he will not spend time discussing the issue at hand. Rather, he empowers his managers to find the solutions and make the decisions. However, he keeps abreast of reports and makes sure he has dashboards that enable him to see and correct where necessary and he has weekly or monthly meetings with all the stakeholders. True leadership is not about control but about creating an environment where others can step into leadership roles with confidence.

It is this approach to leadership that has led to Smily becoming a successful organiser of conferences and training programmes across different countries. He learnt that collaboration was the key to ensuring that each conference or programme was suited to its different context. He describes the successful conference he hosted for the Angello network in India as a *"turning point"*.

"The conference was a turning point, for me, because that

put things in perspective on what's available in the country and what is not, and what different people are doing. So what I realized is there are many other organizations that are doing similar things, like conferences, and they're doing workshops and lots of things. So just after the conference, there was a series of events that let me to think that, and the Lord brought it together, that collaboration is the next thing to do. So how do I take a program that is running somewhere else and collaborate with local leaders to be able to just bring it there."

Throughout his career Smily has faced significant challenges that have shaped his leadership philosophy. One of the most profound lessons came after a major business conference he helped organise. Although the conference was a success, he experienced a fallout with a partner, a situation that could have escalated into long-term resentment. Rather than allow the conflict to damage the relationship permanently, he chose the path of humility and reconciliation and reached out first, prioritising peace over personal grievances.

"If that ... happened a year ago or two years ago, I don't think I would have reacted the same, because it was painful ... The Lord really worked through me. And so there was no ego that jumped up and said, 'You know who you are. You should not be like this.' The Lord made sure that didn't happen. And there was humility that came in. There was no pride like, 'I'm not the one who's going to be reaching out first.' So, I reached out first ... there is always a conscience that we want to keep clear. So that was my main thing ... I want a clear conscience between God and man. Unless you deal with things at this level you're not going to the next level. So that's what the Lord taught me."

Another major challenge has been balancing work, family life, and faith, especially since his wife's businesses is in Dubai. This reality has required intentional effort to maintain family balance. While it would have been easier logistically for one of them to step back, they both recognise that their work is part of a greater calling. Despite the logistical difficulties, they have chosen to continue in their respective roles, knowing that their impact extends beyond their immediate family.

Smily has also learnt that if you make yourself available to the Lord, He will use you whether you feel qualified for that task or not. Your role is to submit in obedience, and He will lead you through.

"That's what I've learned. So, you just have to be available for the Lord and submit to Him in obedience, and he will take you through places you have not imagined. And I've been in that place, and I continue to be in that place and surrender, and as I do that, the Lord is taking me in different places, starting locally, going regional, and then national, and then global. I don't know where this is going, but I want to be made available for the Lord in His time to be able to do what he's calling to do. It doesn't matter my qualification."

Key Themes and Insights

The Evolution of Christian Entrepreneurship in India. Smily highlights a significant shift that is occurring in which Christian entrepreneurs are emerging from church communities to establish businesses. Entrepreneurship is increasingly gaining acceptance within faith communities, with business fellowships, prayer meetings and conferences becoming more common. Churches are now actively supporting entrepreneurs by hosting dedicated gatherings that foster both spiritual and business growth. At the same time, greater access to funding agencies and impact capital is empowering more entrepreneurs to take risks and build sustainable ventures.

"Churches … have business fellowships where businessmen meet once in a month, or, more than that, and then they conduct prayer meeting just for businessmen, and conferences for that. So I'm seeing that happening. And while I grew up, that was not there, and so it was very difficult to even say that you're a businessperson. But right now, it's changing."

Collaboration and Ecosystem Building. Smily advocates for ecosystem-building over individual efforts, emphasising the power of collaboration over competition. Successful collaborations have led to impactful programmes expanding across multiple cities, demonstrating the power of shared vision and partnerships.

"Our primary objective is to glorify the Lord, and the secondary objective is to be connected to people. Our goal is to glorify the Lord … be connected to the Lord. And the secondary objective is to be connected to people."

Smily emphasises that business success is not about individual efforts but about ecosystem-building through collaboration. His role has evolved into that of a connector, bringing organisations together to amplify their impact. By fostering partnerships instead of working in isolation, he has helped expand programmes across multiple cities, demonstrating how a shared vision can drive greater effectiveness and long-term success.

"I don't have to reinvent the wheel if somebody is doing it, let's just partner and make it happen."

Integrating Godly Principles in Business. Business can be a tool for advancing God's kingdom and uplifting communities. Faith is not separate from business; it should shape how entrepreneurs operate and lead. The Acts Community values of humility, generosity and perseverance serve as essential leadership principles, influencing decision-making, stakeholder relationships and long-term impact. Smily shares how integrating these values into business operations ensures that enterprises align with God's purpose, fostering ethical leadership and meaningful transformation.

"It's not about building my kingdom; it's about building His kingdom."

Overcoming Challenges with Humility and Reconciliation. Business challenges, including conflicts, are inevitable, but they must be handled with humility. Smily's decision to choose reconciliation over pride after falling out with a partner reinforced for him the importance of servant leadership, maintaining strong relationships, and prioritising peace over personal gain. Smily's experiences highlight how forgiveness and reconciliation, even in difficult business situations, lead to long-term growth and lasting impact.

Balancing Work, Family, and Faith. Smily and his wife run businesses in different locations; this requires intentional effort to maintain a balance between work and family life. Faith plays a central role in guiding their decisions, ensuring that their work aligns with God's purpose. Their children, witnessing this journey, see business not just as a career but as a calling — an opportunity to serve and create impact.

"If the Lord has put you in a place, that's where the blessing is."

Adapting to Local Contexts for Greater Impact. Programmes and business models need to be contextualised to fit local cultural and economic landscapes. One-size-fits-all approaches do not work. Programmes must be adapted to fit local economic and cultural realities. Smily has seen first-hand how modifying business training programmes with locally relevant case studies makes them more effective. Understanding cultural nuances ensure that initiatives are not only impactful and sustainable but also truly serve the needs of the communities they aim to uplift. Tailoring solutions to specific contexts and communities fosters long-term success and meaningful change.

"What works in India will not work in Singapore, and what works in Singapore probably will not work in Vietnam, because those are all different levels of development, different cultural influences ... those things have to be ironed out ... integrated with the local context."

"I can't give a Singapore example in India and think that, the guy understood everything. I need to give local context ... that is something that Angello really is passionate about, and we want to see that in each of those countries that we operate in. We really like to see local content, local context and local framework."

The Power of Availability and Obedience to God. Success in faith-driven business is not about credentials but about being available for God's work.

"When we are available for the Lord, when we make ourselves available, He uses people who are not really qualified for that particular situation."

Being open to God's calling allows entrepreneurs to grow beyond what they imagined. Many of Smily's achievements stem from obedience to God's leading rather than personal expertise, and his journey is a testament to how this obedience, rather than personal qualifications, leads to unexpected growth and impact. By surrendering to God's plan entrepreneurs can achieve far more than they ever imagined.

Key Principles for Faith-Driven Entrepreneurs

1. Prioritise and Embrace Collaboration

One of the most crucial elements to success in entrepreneurship is to prioritise collaboration. Partnering with existing organisations allows you to leverage their resources, expertise and networks, ultimately creating a foundation for mutual growth and greater impact. By building a network of like-minded individuals and organisations, you not only expand your reach but also create an environment where support is reciprocal, fostering mutual growth and making the work more sustainable and fulfilling.

2. Build Strong Leadership Through Delegation

Empower a second tier of leadership to ensure business continuity and scalability. Building second-tier leadership is a crucial lesson. Delegate with trust, allowing others to take ownership of their responsibilities and grow. Avoid micromanagement by creating a culture of accountability and shared decision-making. By delegating responsibilities and trusting others to lead effectively, you create a stronger, more resilient organisation. Empowering others to step into leadership roles allows you to focus on high-level decisions and vision, while ensuring the operational side of the business continues smoothly. This approach will help build a legacy, as the business is not dependent on one person and can thrive with others leading alongside you.

3. Integrating Faith into Business

In your entrepreneurial journey, integrating faith into business operations is vital. Let the kingdom values of humility, generosity and reconciliation guide every aspect of your business, from operations to leadership. Practising these values in all relationships, including during conflicts, ensures that your decisions and actions align with a greater purpose beyond profits. Approach your business not just as a career but as a calling, keeping your focus on serving others and fulfilling God's greater mission. This approach will enable you to navigate challenges with grace and integrity, knowing that your work is part of a higher purpose.

4. Adapt to Local Contexts and Contextualise Your Approach

Adapting to local contexts is a crucial lesson for any entrepreneur. Every community and every market has its own unique cultural, social and economic realities, and understanding these nuances is vital for tailoring your strategies effectively. One-size-fits-all solutions rarely work; instead, business strategies should be customised to fit the local context. By being mindful of cultural and economic differences you ensure your business remains relevant and can truly meet the needs of the people it serves. Using relatable local examples and stories not only helps you connect with your audience but also makes your offerings more engaging. When your programmes, strategies and messaging resonate with the specific needs of the community, they become more impactful and sustainable in the long term. Contextualising your approach ensures that your initiatives are not only effective but also have a lasting, positive influence on the communities you aim to serve.

5. Balance Work, Family, and Calling

Balancing work and family is a challenge many entrepreneurs face. To maintain a healthy work-life balance, trust and delegate responsibilities to your leadership team. This allows you to focus on strategic decisions and long-term goals while ensuring that day-to-day operations are handled with competence. A clear conscience and prioritising family will help you maintain peace of mind and focus on both your personal and business objectives, ensuring that neither is neglected.

6. Handle Conflict with Humility

Handling conflict with humility is another key lesson for entrepreneurs. In any entrepreneurial journey, conflicts are inevitable. However, reconciliation is the key to sustaining long-term impact. By approaching disagreements with humility and focusing on reconciliation rather than division, you foster healthier relationships and more productive outcomes. This creates a culture of respect and collaboration, even in the face of challenges.

7. Be Available for God's Purpose

Being available for God's work is essential. True success is not just about qualifications and abilities, but about obedience to God's calling. By staying open to God's guidance and aligning your business with His purpose, you ensure that your entrepreneurial endeavours are about more than profit; they become a way to fulfil a higher mission. Success is found in answering God's call and being faithful in your work, knowing that He will guide your steps along the way. Trust that when you make yourself available, God will equip you for the work He has set before you.

8. Stay Rooted in Faith

Staying rooted in faith is vital for maintaining clarity in your decisions. Let your business decisions be guided by God's purpose, rather than purely financial or personal motivations. This will help you navigate challenges with conviction, ensuring that your actions are always aligned with a greater mission. Staying grounded in faith provides a compass that helps you make choices that honour both your values and your entrepreneurial goals.

Reflections on the Angello Network and the Acts Community Values

Smily credits Angello with helping him develop a broader vision for leadership and impact. Before joining the network, he did not see himself as a national leader, but through Angello's mentorship and resources, he gained the confidence to step into that role. One of the aspects he values most about Angello is its ability to identify and nurture leaders at any stage of their journey. He believes that the network's greatest strength lies in its commitment to developing emerging leaders, rather than focusing solely on those who are already well-established.

In addition to leadership development, Smily appreciates Angello's emphasis on contextualising business initiatives. He has observed that many business training programmes in emerging markets fail because they are based on Western models that do not account for local economic and cultural conditions. Angello, however, prioritises the development of local leaders and frameworks, ensuring that programmes are relevant and effective.

> *"When [Angello] found me, I didn't have, actually, any credentials to show that I had a national vision ... That is a capability of Angello ... we still find leaders at any stage during the development and not fully blown leaders when you see them. So that is Angello's core capability."*

The Acts Community model is central to Smily's approach to leadership. He believes that the values emphasising service, generosity and shared purpose should not remain theoretical but should shape daily decision-making, business ethics and relationships. In his view, humility is essential for any leader as success should not lead to ego-inflation or pride but should cultivate a servant-hearted mindset. Generosity is equally important, as a business rooted in faith should prioritise uplifting others rather than focusing on profit. He also stresses the significance of reconciliation, particularly in business conflicts, where treating others with grace and respect can foster stronger relationships and long-term trust.

For Smily, the Acts Community model is not simply about running businesses ethically but about embodying the values of the early church in every aspect of leadership. He notes that challenges such as pride, competition and leadership conflicts are common, but those who follow the Acts Community model can navigate these difficulties by maintaining a posture of humility and selflessness. He believes that leaders must be intentional about cultivating these values, as they do not come naturally but develop through experience and a deep commitment to faith.

> *"For me, Acts Community is a community that is generous, that has humility, that loves each other, that shares between each other. It's very important that leaders have this Acts Community attitude, because as a leader, you are prone to a lot of things. You can be egoistic because that's human nature. Your pride can come in very quickly, because now you are a leader, you have so many followers. People are talking about you. You're on the stage all the time ... you can make lot of enemies as well, because they didn't fall in line."*

"The Acts Community concept ... helps a leader to mould himself, to be Christ-like and to be able to imbibe those values into day to day living, your business, whatever you're doing in terms of kingdom work. Those values are something every leader should follow, and it's not easy. It doesn't come in day one. It is a journey."

Future Vision

Smily envisions a future where Christian entrepreneurs collaborate to scale their impact across India and beyond. He believes that the next phase of growth should not be about establishing new organisations but about facilitating partnerships that enable existing programmes to expand into new regions. His recent efforts have already resulted in the successful introduction of business training programmes in six cities across India, an achievement he hopes to build upon.

Smily emphasises the need to localise business support, recognising that external models often fail when they are not adapted to local cultural and economic realities. He has seen first-hand how modifying business training programmes to include local case studies makes them more effective and relatable. His vision includes expanding these efforts to ensure that Christian entrepreneurs are equipped with the tools they need to succeed in their specific contexts. He also hopes to see more churches embrace entrepreneurship as a legitimate calling, fostering local environments in which business is viewed as a means of serving both God and the community.

"I'm just the connector right now ... operationally, organizations are already there on the ground that can make it happen. God prepares different people for different times and different places. So that is what I've seen. And going forward, that's what I feel should happen, that collaboration should happen at a regional level, at the local level ... it's not about building my kingdom, it's about building His kingdom. So that is where we are heading to."

Closing Reflections on the Conversation

Smily encourages entrepreneurs to embrace faith-driven business, trust in God's timing and remain open to unexpected opportunities. He firmly believes that success is not determined by credentials but by a willingness to be available for God's work. He emphasises that integrating faith into business is not just a theoretical concept but a daily practice that shapes how entrepreneurs lead, make decisions and interact with others.

For those considering stepping into entrepreneurship, Smily offers reassurance that they do not need to have everything figured out. He believes that God equips those He calls and that success comes from obedience rather than expertise. He encourages business leaders to trust that their journey will unfold as they remain faithful to their calling. His experience has shown him that when entrepreneurs align their work with God's purpose, they can achieve far more than they ever imagined.

Generosity with David Harlley and Keren Pybus

Introduction

In this compelling interview, David Harlley and Keren Pybus, both members of the Angello network and committed faith-driven entrepreneurs, reflect on how their deep sense of calling has shaped their respective paths from engineering systems in Canada and fashion sourcing in Bangladesh towards building redemptive, impact-focused enterprises in Africa.

David Harlley is an accomplished business leader with a diverse background spanning engineering, corporate strategy, and impact investment. In addition to his multiple professional roles, he serves as an adjunct lecturer at IE University (Universidad Instituto de Empresa), where he teaches on the topic of Distributive Capitalism, reflecting his commitment to innovative economic models that drive equitable and sustainable impact. David is the CEO of Third Way Capital impact investing firm, which operates in Sub-Saharan Africa. (*See David's bio in Appendix One*)

David spent the first 18 years of his life in Ghana before moving to Canada where he completed a degree in mechanical engineering. It wasn't long before, to use David's word, the Lord "chucked" him into business school, although he had been reluctant because he couldn't "figure out a model for purposeful business." There he learned that there "are, actually, ways to do good things through the marketplace." With the onset of COVID, he teamed up with two partners to "build something that would move capital and expertise into Sub-Saharan Africa," branding themselves as Third Way Capital, an impact firm with "a kingdom mindset … not just how we invest, but how we relate with our partners."

Keren Pybus is the co-founder and CEO of Ethical Apparel Africa (EAA), bringing over 25 years of experience in sourcing, merchandising and retail operations. EAA is an apparel sourcing and manufacturing company with an innovative operating model that prioritizes both product quality and worker well-being. (*See Keren's bio in Appendix One*)

After attaining a degree in fashion, Keren's early career was spent in retail environments. It was while running a sourcing office in Bangladesh that she observed the impact of that environment on workers. An opportunity arose to move to Africa, and it was in South Africa that she "had a very strong calling from God … two very independent prophetic words around if you want to walk on the water, you have got to get out of the boat." However, she delayed doing anything about until she was made redundant.

> "So, God literally kicked me out the boat because he got fed up with waiting for me to make a move." – Keren.

At that time, she was receiving life-coaching from a Christian woman who helped her understand that her calling lay where her passion and skills collided. Her skills and passion lay in the manufacturing clothing industry, but her heart was for the workers - how to get more money to the workers, how to create sustainable jobs, and how to use jobs in the marketplace as a route out of poverty. In thinking through this process, Keren "*ended up in Ghana on a different programme and found this incredible country with all these incredible people and this incredible opportunity to grow an industry.*" Within a short space of time, she had co-founded EAA and 10 years later they have a factory with 750 workers and "*the incredible opportunity to have investment.*"

Keren and David's stories are marked by obedience, risk and a shared commitment to Kingdom values. Their partnership was formed when Third Way Capital invested in Keren's company. Their reflections in this conversation reveal how capital and compassion can converge to fuel purpose-driven business, inviting fellow entrepreneurs to re-think business as a platform for justice, dignity, sustainability and spiritual transformation.

Leadership and Impact

David and Keren lead with an unwavering commitment to faith-driven principles. Their leadership is not about position or prestige; it's about purpose and calling. David channels capital and expertise into Sub-Saharan Africa, seeking redemptive returns that go beyond profit. Keren champions worker welfare and systemic change in the apparel industry in Ghana. Both see leadership as a response to God's call to serve others through business.

When David and his business partner in Third Way Capital heard about Keren's story and her calling it was an obvious match.

"It certainly makes it a lot easier when you have a common language around what it is you're actually trying to achieve, so that you're not just tracking business metrics … you're tracking spiritual metrics." – David.

David leads relationally. Businesses are run by people, so emotional intelligence is necessary to connect with them.

"We're going to figure out much more about people than we are going to figure out about the business. And I strongly believe that most businesses will sink or swim based on who's running them." – David.

David and his partners consider empathy to be their company's "superpower", believing that developing genuine care beyond the business relationship not only stands them in better stead for any challenges that may arise, it also allows them to enjoy their work a lot more.

When Keren and David connected, Keren's company had reached the point where they needed institutionalized investment with an investor who wants to be actively involved and interested in the impact aspect of their work.

"To know that from the beginning we were going to be held accountable to our impact as much as our financial return, excited us." – Keren.

Keren exemplifies humility in leadership. She shares candidly about never aspiring to be a CEO and the steep learning curve of building a business. Her openness to admit what she doesn't know, lean on others' strengths and lead collaboratively has created a culture of trust and empowerment in her company. To find an investor who recognizes that EAA's mission is to invest profits back into its workers, and that growth is measured in terms of jobs created rather than financial return to shareholders, was a great relief.

"And so to find a company that were like pushing us in that area, by pushing our impact goals and pushing our people development goals, and, you know, putting people at the centre of what we did, was a relief as much as it was an excitement, because I was terrified of going down that kind of next road." – Keren.

For both leaders, success cannot be measured by financial returns alone. They measure impact through dignity restored, jobs created, lives transformed, and communities uplifted. These are the *"spiritual metrics"* that David applies, the change that reveals Kingdom impact at work.

Under Keren's leadership, her business does more than meet ethical standards; it actively pursues redemption, socially and spiritually. She prioritizes the needs of her 750 workers, most of whom are women, ensuring fair wages, stability and holistic wellbeing. Her vision is to create a secure, spiritually grounded workplace that builds community.

"Most people go to work every day. And how about if that workplace is a place that is secure. It's safe. It's a place that

enables you to grow, enables your family to grow. It enables you to grow spiritually, enables you to grow mentally, enables you to grow physically. Enables your brain to grow, enables you to develop community relationships and it equips you to then do what Jesus would have done to then bless others, to be able to then pass that forward, to be able to share your knowledge and your skills with other people." – Keren.

EAA is not marketed as a Christian business, although Keren states it is obvious to anyone who interacts with them that Christian values are intrinsic to the way decisions are taken in the organisation. Much of their support comes from people and countries of diverse cultures and religions. They have a weekly staff meditation session that can be led by people of different faiths, and Keren ensures that prayer is central to everything they do. Keren ensures that EAA is a place where workers have dignity and purpose, producing apparel that is truly needed - workwear, underwear, and clothing designed for everyday life.

"Why not utilize the fact that we all go to work to create something that is going to be redemptive to people, and alongside make some great clothes and equip people? Yeah, we make it a really big point that we try and make things that people need, not want." – Keren.

David and Keren are committed to improving the lives of those their enterprises touch. David's investments have brought new possibilities to under-served regions, while Keren's company has tangibly improved livelihoods in Ghana. Their influence extends beyond their organizations into broader ecosystems of faith-driven change. Recognizing the challenges of leadership, both David and Keren intentionally cultivate supportive, prayerful communities around them. These relationships, ranging from mentors and fellow entrepreneurs to family and faith groups, play a critical role in sustaining their vision and wellbeing.

David and Keren offer a compelling vision of leadership marked by courage, compassion, integrity and faith. Their lives serve as a blueprint for others seeking to lead businesses that are not only profitable but are also purposeful and transformative.

Challenges and Lessons

Operating in Ghana and Sub-Saharan Africa brings many challenges, from currency instability to logistical hurdles. Yet both David and Keren remain committed to doing business the right way, even when it costs more or takes longer. They choose redemptive action over convenience, constantly asking what's best for their employees and communities.

David describes how, when aggressive devaluation of the Ghanaian Cedi occurred in Ghana between 2021 and 2024, EAA was quick to evaluate what that would mean for the business and its pay structure and apply the necessary holistic action for sustainability, rather than having to be pressured into doing so by their investment partners.

"So it's obviously a relief when you are in with a business where that ... spiritual or Kingdom framing of what good business is common language, it's common on both sides ... 'How do we make this happen in a way that it doesn't jeopardize the business?' ... And so, you know, the adjustments get made, obviously, with the right amount of common sense ... because they're not running a charity anymore, they're running a business, and they make some business decisions, but do not limit themselves to ... what's the least we can do to clear the line? But rather, what's best for these women, not just at the factory, but at the level of their homes? What's happening in their homes?" – David.

David points to the importance of being *"wary of the easy answer"* because *"God is in the details."*

"... sometimes we look for the easy explanation, for ... a set of social dynamics, a way to check the box and say, 'I did the right thing', but really getting your hands dirty and

understanding the pain point of who you're working with ... that's how you make actual change. That's how you make actual impact happen." – David.

David and Keren candidly acknowledge the fear and uncertainty that come with stepping out in faith. Keren describes being *"kicked out of the boat"* when she was made redundant, interpreting it as God's way of urging her into a new chapter in a region where, as David explains, there are *"all kinds of resource limitations."* The learning is that they are never going to do things perfectly, but the intention must be to do the best with what they have. Keren's advises that it's also important to admit to one' own shortcomings:

".. really being clear and admitting what you can and can't do ... one person is not going to be able to run an entire organization with every perfect skill that you need to do all of those things." – Keren.

Keren shares that although she has decades of experience visiting factories and knows what a successful garment factory looks like, running one herself has required a new level of humility and willingness to ask for help. At Ethical Apparel Africa, she relies heavily on her co-founder Paloma, whose expertise in compliance, finance, and HR complements Keren's strengths in production and technical operations. She emphasizes the importance of internal and external collaboration and of admitting to one's own vulnerability.

"So ... surround yourself with advisors, with people that you can bounce ideas off, people that you can speak to, and that it's okay even when you're the leader, to be vulnerable within those conversations, to admit when you don't know things, and you know, even with your team, who know you're hiring a set, a team of experts that know more than you do on a lot of subjects, and to utilize that and be humble within that." - Keren

Faith is a constant anchor in moments of risk and doubt. Keren and David stress the importance of trusting God and being surrounded by people who will pray, encourage, and walk alongside. Prayer is critically important.

"... having a prayer network that's going to support you ... I have an incredible network of people that are on their knees praying for what we're doing ... and when things happen like USAID getting cancelled." – Keren.

Keren refers to her parents' small prayer group - retired individuals with little exposure to Africa or apparel manufacturing yet faithfully interceding in prayer continually. She also values the insight of her husband, whose creativity and spiritual grounding provide perspectives she might not otherwise see.

"So I'll take him something, and he will come up with a solution I will never ever have thought of in a million years ... it doesn't work in business ... but that doesn't mean that you can't hear from God and hear things that maybe sometimes you get blocked from because you're so in it." – Keren.

Networks of faith-driven entrepreneurs, such as Faith Driven Entrepreneur, Faith in Business (for whom she is a trustee) and Angello provide peer support, wisdom, and theological framing to navigate the practical and spiritual challenges of running an impact business. For Keren, leadership is about trusting that God provides both people and pathways.

"Walking on the water is fixing your eyes on Jesus ..." – Keren.

David reflects that perhaps his biggest challenge is the fear of loneliness.

I think it all comes down to that ... Will there be anyone with me? Will I be alone? And often in the Bible, you know God is saying, 'Be strong and courageous. I will be with you.' And how He shows up is through people. It's through the communities that He helps us build in places that we didn't think would be there." – David.

David frames community as the antidote to loneliness by stressing that loneliness accompanies leadership. He recommends that if you feel you are being called "to step out of the boat" look for the support "because more than likely it is there," whether that be temporary or long-term, formal or informal. He refers to the work and its supporting community as the "incarnation" of Kingdom work being done. The work itself should be transformational both for you and the communities you are involved with. Transformation begins with relationships.

"Relationship is one of the primary tools that God uses to change hearts and minds." – David.

Furthermore, "*stepping out of the boat*" induces fear, and if there is no fear "*maybe that's not where you're supposed to be.*"

"Do something that scares you … whatever it is, it should keep you up at night, at least a little bit, because then that's a gap that allows God to step in and create that change." – David.

Beyond his investment work, David has written a book on '*distributive capitalism*,' a phrase he coined while designing a course for his university, which refers to an economic framework rooted in decentralizing ownership and dispersing opportunity as opposed to the oligopoly of concentrated wealth and large monopolies that squeeze out small businesses, dispersed ownership and a more democratic marketplace. David argues that true democracy is impossible without democratizing the marketplace because the marketplace affects everyday life. Currently, lobby groups protecting their wealth dictate how we experience our lives. He believes that models of shared ownership, where employees and communities hold meaningful stakes in enterprises, are critical for the future. His book seeks not only to present these ideas but to spark conversation about how capitalism itself can evolve to reflect justice, equity and sustainability.

So, yeah, hopefully ... this gains some traction, but the big thing for me is, let's have a conversation. Let's not assume that neo-liberal capitalism is the end of it all, and we can never have anything evolved beyond that ... if this book invites conversation, then half the job's done." – David.

Together, Keren and David embody a model of leadership grounded in humility, strengthened by community, and fuelled by a shared belief that business is both relational and redemptive. Their journey illustrates that redemptive entrepreneurship demands courage, community, sacrifice, and a lifelong posture of learning.

Key Themes and Insights

Faith and Calling. David and Keren attribute the pivots made in their careers to deep, faith-driven callings. David, who originally trained as a mechanical engineer in Canada, felt compelled to return to Ghana and eventually entered the world of impact investing through what he describes as being "chucked" into business school by God. Keren, whose career began in global fashion sourcing, received prophetic words that sparked a major shift, ultimately leading her to found a redemptive manufacturing business in Ghana.

"If you want to walk on the water, you have got to get out of the boat." – Keren.

Purpose Over Profession. Neither David nor Keren began their careers envisioning their current roles, but both were driven by a desire to do work that truly mattered. David struggled to find a purposeful business model until he discovered a business school with a humanities-centred approach. Keren's passion for just treatment of women workers led her to establish a business focused on sustainable job creation and dignity for factory workers.

"My heart was … how do you get more money to the workers? How do you create sustainable jobs? How do you use jobs in the marketplace as a route out of poverty?" – Keren.

Redemptive Business, Not Just Ethical Business. Both leaders go beyond ethical compliance, aiming instead for redemptive practices that address systemic injustices and place people at the centre of enterprise. This includes proactively responding to currency devaluation, addressing gender dynamics in the workforce, and creating solutions that positively impact the home lives of workers.

"Being redemptive in the way that we work, not just ethical." – Keren.

"God is in the details." – David.

Relationships Drive Impact. The strength of David and Keren's partnership lies in shared values and deep relational trust. David describes relationship-building as the core of Third Way Capital's approach to investment, where empathy and emotional intelligence take precedence over traditional metrics. Keren adds that this relational support through mentors, prayer networks and peer communities is vital to sustaining faith and vision in the face of uncertainty.

"Our superpower … is empathy … emotional intelligence and the ability to connect with people." – David.

Community and Support Networks. Both leaders emphasise the necessity of surrounding themselves with people who will intercede with prayer and wisdom. Whether it's Keren's parents' small group or David's broader spiritual and entrepreneurial circles, they agree that no one is called to walk this journey alone.

"God shows up through people. It's through the communities He helps us build." – David.

Key Principles for Faith-Driven Entrepreneurs

1. Lead with Vulnerability and Humility

Keren openly shares that she did not set out to be a CEO, yet through faith and obedience she found herself leading a thriving manufacturing business. She emphasizes the value of surrounding yourself with skilled people and admitting what you don't know, remaining teachable throughout the journey. Leadership, in her view, is not about having all the answers but creating space for others to contribute meaningfully.

2. Integrate Faith Authentically into Business

Faith is fully woven into the culture of David and Keren's enterprises. From prayer meetings in the Ghana office to multi-faith meditation sessions and company-wide prayer networks, both leaders make space for spiritual discernment in everyday operations. Their decisions, big and small, are filtered through a commitment to listening for God's guidance.

3. Redefine Success Through Kingdom Metrics

Profitability is not the only metric that matters. Both David and Keren stress the importance of evaluating impact through a Kingdom lens: Job creation, worker wellbeing, ethical treatment and spiritual transformation are all part of the equation.

"You're not just tracking business metrics ... you're tracking spiritual metrics." – David.

4. Prioritize Empathy and Emotional Intelligence

David sees empathy as a business superpower. At Third Way Capital, emotional intelligence is essential, not only in evaluating partners but also in sustaining meaningful relationships that drive long-term impact. Understanding the lived realities of workers, clients and communities shape how both leaders approach business decisions.

5. Champion Sustainability and Worker Welfare

Keren's business model is intentionally built around creating long-term, sustainable jobs, especially for women in Ghana. She advocates producing what people need rather than what they want, ensuring that workers are not only paid fairly but are also supported holistically in their wellbeing and growth.

6. Surround Yourself with Prayerful, Supportive Community

David and Keren do not recommend trying to lead alone. Both lean on a strong network of mentors, advisors and prayer partners. Whether it's a retired prayer group or a spouse with a totally different perspective, they affirm the vital role of spiritual and emotional support.

Reflections on the Angello Network and the Acts Community Values

David Harlley and Keren Pybus embody the spirit of the early Church as reflected in the Book of Acts, where community, shared purpose and faith-led generosity were central. Through their connection with the Angello network and other movements such as Faith Driven Investor, Faith Driven Entrepreneur and Faith in Business, they have found communities that share their language of faith, impact and redemptive enterprise. Their leadership is grounded in the belief that business is not a solo pursuit but a communal endeavour where prayer, empathy and shared values cultivate transformation at every level.

Within their own organizations, David and Keren actively foster environments of care, prayer and spiritual grounding. In Ghana, Keren's team begins each week with prayer and hosts regular meditation sessions that welcome all faiths, reinforcing a culture of inclusivity and respect. These practices are central to how decisions are made and how people are treated.

David and Keren reflect deeply on Angello's overarching mission, emphasizing that true success lies not just in financial returns but in Kingdom impact, transforming lives, communities and business cultures. For them, spiritual metrics matter.

The Angello network exists to empower faith-driven entrepreneurs by offering resources, mentoring and a community of like-minded peers. The achievements of David and Keren are examples of what is possible when faith, business acumen and relational support come together. Their journey illustrates the Angello network's goal to enable business leaders to thrive both spiritually and professionally.

Angello's impact goes far beyond capital deployment. It's a faith-fuelled ecosystem that views business as a tool for redemptive change. For David and Keren, this means holding themselves to Kingdom standards while also leaning into the strength and wisdom of a trusted community.

Their example captures Angello's heartbeat: Activating capital, talent and conviction for redemptive enterprise, and doing so with courage, clarity, and compassion.

Future Vision

David and Keren are united in their ambition to expand the reach and influence of their work geographically, relationally and spiritually. For Keren, the focus is on deepening her company's impact in Ghana and beyond, continuing to create sustainable jobs, investing in worker development and ensuring that people remain at the heart of business growth. David's vision extends to re-shaping economic systems themselves. Through his upcoming book and ongoing work with Third Way Capital, he promotes the concept of 'Distributive Capitalism,' a framework for decentralizing ownership, spreading opportunity and democratizing the marketplace.

"Unless we can democratize the marketplace through these sorts of means and methods, we won't have full democracy."
– David.

Both leaders envision business ecosystems that reflect the justice, generosity and creativity of God. They aim to set an example for how faith-driven values, when truly integrated, can lead to thriving enterprises that bless people and communities. Faith will remain central to everything they do. As they scale, David and Keren are determined not to compromise on the spiritual principles that define their leadership. Prayer, discernment, integrity and a commitment to people will continue to guide decisions at every level.

Their shared vision is bold: To create and support businesses that do not simply survive in difficult environments but lead a movement of redemptive entrepreneurship - businesses that heal, empower and transform.

Closing Reflections on the Conversation

This conversation stands as a powerful testimony to how faith can shape enterprise, leadership, and systems. David and Keren's insights offer a compelling invitation to entrepreneurs everywhere:

- Step out in faith even when it feels uncertain.
- Prioritize people over profit.
- Build holistically, with community and spiritual alignment.
- Let your business be a vessel for redemption.

David and Keren's reflections underscore the profound impact that integrating faith into business can have. They encourage fellow entrepreneurs to trust in God, build strong, ethical relationships and champion sustainable, people-centred practices that reflect Kingdom values. Their stories are inspirational, demonstrating that Godly principles translate into successful, impactful business operations.

"If you're doing things that don't cause you to feel fear, then they're beneath you. So whatever it is, it should keep you up at night, at least a little bit, because then that's a gap that allows God to step in and create that change." - David.

"Why not utilize the fact that we all go to work to create something that is going to be redemptive to people?" - Keren.

Joy with Mason Tan

Introduction

A graduate of the University of Southern California with a B.Sc. and a Master's degree in Accounting, Mason Tan has worked across the U.S., Indonesia, Singapore, and China. Mason is a pioneer in social impact investing in Asia. In 2013, he co-founded Garden Impact Investments Pte Ltd and Transformational Business Network Asia (TBN Asia), both of which focus on addressing poverty through sustainable business solutions. Mason also serves on the global board of directors of Prison Fellowship International (PFI), leveraging his expertise in finance, accounting and impact investing to drive innovative approaches to blended economic development and social transformation.

Mason Tan is a U.S. Certified Public Accountant with over 35 years of international experience in finance and entrepreneurship. As the Director of Impact Investing at Providentia Wealth Advisory, a regulated fund manager in Singapore, he oversees the Garden Impact Fund, supporting scalable businesses that drive social change, focusing primarily in Southeast Asia.

In this interview Mason shares how he transitioned from a corporate life centred on profit to a purpose-driven, socially impactful entrepreneurial path. The turning point came in what he calls a "quarter-life crisis" at the age of 35 when he "accepted the Lord," coming to realise that God cares about humanity and that life is "more than just work." Mason describes himself as having been "a slave to the corporate profit greed system." Yet, after some years as a church-going Christian, he realised there was little transformation in his life and began reading the Bible seriously from beginning to end.

> "God ... led me through this transformation journey to become a born again Christian and helped me to take a deep dive through the 66 books in the Bible."

Studying the bible in its entirety became a life-transforming journey that helped him understand what "God's heartbeat is all about." He reflected deeply about what it means to be a disciple of Jesus and to become more Christ-like. This process of inner transformation led to a change in values, and he became intentional about how to serve God both in the church and in the marketplace.

As a member of the Angello network, Mason exemplifies stewardship, integrity and sustainable impact, demonstrating how faith-based principles can seamlessly translate into business success. His experiences highlight the power of integrating faith into entrepreneurship, fostering genuine relationships and maintaining a vision that extends beyond profit.

Mason shares his insights on balancing purpose and profit, the role of faith and perseverance in business, and the importance of true relational and reciprocal community. His story offers invaluable lessons for fellow entrepreneurs on navigating challenges, fostering meaningful collaborations, and leading with integrity.

Leadership and Impact

Mason Tan expresses a deep conviction that God's purpose for him and all genuinely Christ-centred investors is to be "marketplace stewards, the bridge between the marketplace and the church" by bringing the values of Jesus into the marketplace. Mason believes his God-given talent in finance gives him a specific role to play in linking church and marketplace. He advocates three key changes:

1. A shift away from profit-driven business practice to purpose-driven.

The guiding principles for purpose-driven investment is to be intentional about using capital as a resource to help grow businesses that can transform and benefit the society, instead of merely a profit-generating vehicle.

2. A shift away from shareholder capitalism to stakeholder capitalism.

Stakeholder capitalism means recognizing there must be more than just profit for shareholders or owners; there must be intentional impact that leads to human flourishing for all those contributing to, and connected to, the business in its social context, including for the employees, the customers, the vendors and the communities where the businesses are located.

3. A shift away from profit maximizing to profit optimizing.

Profit optimizing involves looking for projects that will grow organically, allowing all the stakeholders to profit along with it. Mason's commitment to "human flourishing" comes from his understanding of the four major themes in the Bible: Creation (with human beings in God's image tasked with stewardship of it), Sin, Redemption, and Restoration. Redemption has already been achieved for us by Jesus on the cross. Restoration is the process of being restored to holiness – to the people God created us to be in His image as revealed in Jesus Christ. It's here that we have our part to play: It involves accountability, "carrying the cross of Jesus" as we strive for holiness.

"And that's not just appearance, but your heart, your behaviour and your ways of pursuing it. This we call the pursuit of holiness ... being very intentional about applying what you learn in the Bible ... in terms of showing patience, grace and mercies, etc."

For Mason, *"living out what you believe"* in pursuit of holiness is "spiritual leadership," and because there is *"always a tension between what God calls us to do and what the world demands us to do"* it is important to seek out others who are similarly convicted. He identifies three aspects to spiritual leadership:

- **Stewardship** – "recognize that everything that is in our hands actually belongs to God. We don't own anything out of it. And recognizing we need to do things according to what God want us to do, because all belongs to him."
- **Servanthood** – "when God puts you in a position of authority, you're supposed to serve the people and demonstrate that as a servant, you serve people below you, not just above you."
- **Self-Sacrifice** – "giving up your own desire, giving up your own personal goals to be in line to carry the Jesus cross … to live out the holiness."

In his determination to "walk the talk," Mason, together with Dr Kim Tan, founded the Garden Impact Investments in late 2013, which subsequently was known as Garden Impact Fund. The name of the Fund alludes to the perfect world in Genesis before the fall, and Eden restored as described in Revelation Ch. 22. He recalls the skepticism and hesitancy surrounding the initiative because at that time, in 2013, very few people understood what social impact was and were even doing social impact investing. However, Isaiah Ch. 58 was very much on his heart, and he was aware that all the Jewish biblical festivals were about God's desire to free humanity from the bondage of sin and darkness in the world.

"With that understanding of the theme of fighting poverty, all our investors understand that there must be a better way to help the poor and the needy people than by just giving them money as charity or grants."

The investors Mason and Kim identified to support the Fund committed themselves to investing in those who had fallen on hard times or lacked opportunity.

"Our investment is really targeting businesses that will

lift the so-called vulnerable people out of poverty. It's not about charity; it's about giving them a sustainable economic livelihood so that they can become financially independent."
"And so, by being involved in an organization like Angello or even by an NGO like Prison Fellowship International, we recognize that everyone deserves a second chance, third chance, fourth chance, fifth chance, just as God has redeemed us regardless of how many times we have failed him."

Mason's leadership is grounded in faith, exhibiting humility, resilience and service. He leads by example, fostering a workplace culture where social impact is prioritised over personal gain. His approach to leadership encourages others to adopt a similar mindset, recognising the importance of contributing to the greater good rather than pursuing individual success.

"A lot of people enjoy power. A lot of people enjoy position. But actually when God puts you in a high position of authority, you're supposed to serve the people."

Mason's leadership is shaped by his determination to live and lead with intentionality and impact. Beyond his innovative leadership, Mason actively engages in mentorship, guiding aspiring entrepreneurs on how to integrate their faith into their professional lives, helping them to navigate the challenges of balancing purpose with profit.

Further, Mason extends his influence on a global scale as a board member of Prison Fellowship International. In this role, he helps drive rehabilitation programmes beyond the prison cells that uplift and transform communities worldwide, demonstrating his commitment to use his expertise and resources to invest in creating positive change beyond the traditional business world.

"The first thing we look at is actually, 'How is this business going to lead people out of poverty, and what are the beneficiary groups?' At Garden Impact Fund level, we look at five so-

called vulnerable target groups: First, are the incarcerated. Second are the refugees and migrant workers. Third are survivors of human trafficking and domestic violence. The fourth are the farmers and those who are daily wage workers, because they are the most prone to loan sharks. And the last group that we are very interested in are special needs adults. Why do we say that? Because all these people, I believe God also loves them as much as He loves us."

Mason emphasizes that faith-driven leadership comes from the heart, together with a mindset to pursue the goal of human flourishing against all odds.

"The reward is really fascinating, in terms of they become financially independent but more importantly, they become productive citizens of the community."

Mason cites the Agape Contact Centre inside the men's prison Changi prison in Singapore as a case in point. It began as a call centre within the prison that initially employed 15 people and generated revenue of less than $200 US dollars a year. In 12 years, it grew into a business with revenue of $4 million. The call centre has now expanded to outside the prison where they employ released prisoners. They also recruit single mothers, wheelchair bound people, and the elderly. Many of the employees are working not just for the money - they are working so that they can restore the broken relationships with their loved ones. The Agape Contact Centre is now much more than a call centre – it's a restoration centre with multiple services. These include an employment agency, a digital marketing agency, and a learning academy with training programmes such as the Agape Transformation Programme which transforms lives by empowering people to overcome self-limiting beliefs, enhance self-awareness and take ownership of gaining employment.

"That restoration journey, restoring the brokenness with their loved ones, the trust, the credibility, is such an important journey that we realized that, you know, we need to do more,

more and more."

Another example of the impact made by Garden Impact Fund investments is Greenhope, a world leader in developing biodegradable products to reduce plastic pollution. What began as an enterprise sourcing cassava starch from a farmer cooperative of fewer than 200 farmers, now purchases cassava from cooperatives of approximately 3000 farmers under fair trade schemes. Greenhope's products have replaced over 150,000 tons of conventional plastic, equivalent to 12.7 billion plastic bags. In this way, Greenhope is driving economic empowerment in rural communities, providing economic livelihood opportunities and measurable improvements in the living conditions of farmers and their families. When Mason and his partners became involved, Greenhope's revenue was approximately $300,000 US per annum; this has increased to $8 million.

Mason's commitment to purpose-driven investing has guided the Fund's strategic decisions, shaping its high-touch, socially transformative approach to empower organisations to address systemic issues and deliver measurable social benefits.

Challenges and Lessons

Following the spiritual transformation that led Mason into the *"second part"* of his Christian life, he committed himself to bring the values of Jesus into the marketplace and to apply them through his God-given talents in finance for the purpose of social upliftment. But this path is strewn with challenges, and it requires faith and resilience.

"... for spiritual leadership, you know, you need to live out what, what you believe."

Isaiah 58: 6 -10 is his guiding scripture passage: 'Is not this the kind of fasting I have chosen: to loosen the chains of injustice ... to set the oppressed free ... Is it not to share your food with the hungry?' Mason stresses the importance of discerning "*true fasting*" when evaluating potential partners.

Evaluating the right partners for social impact investment is a challenging responsibility. It requires a relational approach that goes beyond the level of personal involvement required by conventional investment metrics. Mason sets clear social impact KPIs, but he is also conscious that the responsibility of discernment and oversight requires continual awareness of the fact that every Christian, including himself, is on a journey of restoration. Because of this, he endeavours to remain intentional about extending the biblical values of patience, grace and mercy.

"We recognize that everyone deserves a second chance, third chance, fourth chance, fifth chance — just as how God has redeemed us, regardless of how many times we have failed Him."

Mason stresses that social impact investors must know that it's not about financial rewards; it's about how to allow God to work in your life so that you can be a steward for human flourishing.

"In our journey, we learn to pray a lot. We learn to really seek out what God's will for this business is."

A typical private equity investment deal considers the financial potential of an enterprise first, but the first thing the Garden Impact Fund partners examine before investing are the potential beneficiaries and whether the enterprise can raise people out of poverty. Mason points out that often the enterprises they work with require a "high touch" approach, but the reward comes in seeing them become financially independent productive citizens in their communities and passing that gift on to others.

"Most of the social entrepreneurs, while they have a passion for what they are doing in terms of helping vulnerable groups, they are not that financially savvy, and because of the size, the

scale of the business, they can't afford to hire a proper CFO or financial savvy people, so as an investor, we are most likely required to be involved in a high touch approach, meaning really have to help them to set up the business strategy, cash flow management, you know, helping them to assess whether debt or equity for future fundraising is more reasonable."

"To really make your investment work in a social enterprise, you need to adopt a high touch approach."

Mason emphasises the importance of ensuring that you are investing in entrepreneurs who *"have the right heart,"* and stresses the importance of patience in social impact investing.

"When I say patient … I mean really patient. I still remember about 20 years ago a normal commercial economic cycle ranged between 8 to 10 years, but today we're looking at 3 years. I think a meaningful exit for any social impact investor should be between 10 to 15 years. They must be prepared to have that patience and the risk appetite to … actually see changes in the community, lifting people out of poverty."

It becomes very difficult when the investor and the investee do not share the same values. There is ongoing tension to be navigated between profit-driven and purpose-driven business practices and aligning investor expectations with social impact goals. Mason notes the challenge of managing not only the investee, but also the investor.

"During the past 12 years, we have learned a lot of some of the potential pitfalls. You know, a lot of people use the traditional investing hat to do social impact investing, and unfortunately, that is a path to failure."

"I must warn those who are looking for a quick box return, you'll be very disappointed."

In Mason's worldview, social impact investors are stewards. Mason emphasizes that stewardship is about accountability – accountability to God, accountability to yourself, and accountability to others.

> "Accountability to God means, 'Am I following my Shepherd's Voice?' Accountability to self means 'Am I just a paper Christian or am I a true follower of Jesus Christ?' Accountability to others means 'Do I have a heart for the poor?'"

Social entrepreneurship is fraught with obstacles, and Mason's successes reveal that resilience comes from faith and a strong sense of purpose. When challenges arise, they are to be viewed as opportunities for growth rather than setbacks. Mason acknowledges that the investment landscape is complex, and he thinks deeply about the dynamics involved.

> "The new generation of investors are more demanding ... more accountability, more transparency. Which is good. This will make sure the expectations align in terms of not just financial, but also the impact outcome and impact output. Honestly, I think we are in a period of transition whereby we see an intergenerational transfer of wealth, and we need to be more mindful about some of the expectations these asset owners have in mind."

This holistic, considered perspective shapes Mason's leadership and investing philosophy. Redemption and restoration are not just spiritual concepts; they are practical business values, founded upon faith, hope and love.

> "I would say that as followers of Jesus Christ, we are called to be faithful stewards of all the gifts God gives us, including time, talents and treasures. To demonstrate that you are able to do good and do well at the same time. And I think this is something that many Christians are struggling with. How can I do good and do well at the same time? There's no right or wrong way ... It's just that, you know God, God is amazing."

Key Themes and Insights

Faith, Transformation, and Purpose-Driven Business. Mason's journey began with a realisation that his corporate life lacked deeper meaning. Accepting Christ at 35, he initially thought his mission was complete with church attendance and tithing. However, he later recognised the need for a profound inner transformation, leading him to read the entire Bible and seek God's greater purpose for his life. This shift redefined his business philosophy, moving from profit-driven to purpose-driven business practices. He emphasises stakeholder capitalism over shareholder capitalism, viewing business as a tool for societal benefit rather than mere profit generation.

"I started to shift away from profit-driven to purpose-driven. That's number one. Number two is shifting away from shareholder capitalism to stakeholder capitalism. And number three is to shift away from profit maximizing to profit optimizing. These are the three key changes that I personally feel very convicted about right now ... with what's God's calling is for me."

Spiritual Leadership and Stewardship in Business. Mason emphasises the importance of spiritual leadership, stewardship and servant leadership in business. He believes that everything belongs to God and that leaders are elected to serve others, not for personal gain. This perspective shapes his approach to decision-making and team leadership.

"Stewardship is recognising that everything in our hands actually belongs to God. We don't own anything."

Building Relationships Based on Trust and Mutual Growth. Mason values relationships over financial transactions, echoing Angello's philosophy of "connection without control." He believes that trust, shared values and mutual growth form the foundation of successful collaborations.

The Acts Community Values in Business. Mason integrates the Angello's Acts Community values of fellowship, discipleship, joy, generosity, service and impact into his leadership approach. He believes these values are fundamental to ethical business practices and long-term impact.

Overcoming Challenges with Purpose and Resilience. Entrepreneurship is fraught with obstacles, but Mason views challenges as opportunities for growth. Mason highlights the difficulty of aligning investor expectations with social impact goals and emphasises the importance of accountability to God, to oneself, and to others.

Impact Investing with Integrity and Love. As a co-founder of the Garden Impact Fund, Mason is dedicated to impact investing that empowers vulnerable groups, lifting them out of poverty.

"I think most people have the misperception saying that the poor are where they are because they are lazy. But I beg to differ, most people remain poor because of lack of opportunities that we have received."

He advocates for high-touch approaches and patience in social impact investing, emphasising empowerment over handouts. Mason's approach counters scarcity thinking by treating vulnerable groups as capable partners in transformation, not passive recipients of aid.

"It's not about charity; it's about giving them a sustainable economic livelihood so that they can become financially independent ... how we can help these people to achieve in a so-called financially sustainable manner."

Future Vision: Empowering the Next Generation. Mason is passionate about mentoring and equipping the next generation of entrepreneurs to build businesses that prioritise people, purpose and impact. He believes that by sharing knowledge and resources, business leaders can create a ripple effect of positive transformation.

"It's not about helping the rich to become richer. It's really more about helping vulnerable groups of people to achieve

financial independence over an extended period of time. That's what excites me."

Key Principles for Faith-Driven Entrepreneurs

1. Doing Good and Doing Well: A Bridge Between Church and Marketplace.

Mason Tan emphasizes a core principle that sits at the heart of faith-driven entrepreneurship: The ability to do good (i.e.: pursue redemptive, socially impactful, Kingdom outcomes) and do well (i.e.: achieve financial sustainability and excellence) at the same time. He challenges the common tension many Christians feel between purpose and profit, affirming that these two goals are not mutually exclusive. Instead, mission and margin can and should coexist, reframed as an opportunity, not a contradiction.

"I think what one hopes to do is to demonstrate that you are able to do good and do well at the same time."

This mindset invites Christian business leaders to steward their resources with excellence, operate with unwavering integrity, and serve their communities, while also building resilient, scalable enterprises. Mason sees faith-driven entrepreneurs as bridges carrying the values, compassion and redemptive vision of the Church into the marketplace. He believes this bridging role is a calling, a form of discipleship that connects two often-separated spheres for mutual transformation.

"I believe as marketplace believers, or even stewards, that we are called to be the bridge between the marketplace and the church."

In this view, business becomes a mission field and a ministry, a place where believers live out their faith, model Christlike leadership and bring healing and hope through enterprise. Together, these principles position entrepreneurs not only as builders of businesses, but as culture-shapers, system reformers and Kingdom ambassadors in the modern economy.

2. Integrate Faith into Business.
Apply biblical principles in daily business operations, focusing on serving others and prioritising purpose over profit. A business aligned with faith and values creates lasting impact.

3. Embrace Stewardship.
Recognise that all resources, whether financial, relational, or intellectual, ultimately belong to God. Use them responsibly and with a heart for service, ensuring they contribute to the greater good.

4. Build Authentic Relationships.
Trust and mutual respect are the foundation of strong business connections. Prioritise long-term, values-driven relationships over short-term, transactional interactions.

5. Practice Patience and a High-Touch Approach.
Success, particularly in social impact ventures, takes time. Be actively involved in guiding businesses toward sustainable growth, recognising that transformation requires commitment.

6. Focus on Human Flourishing.
Business should elevate human dignity. Create opportunities that empower vulnerable communities and provide pathways to economic independence.

7. Lead with Integrity and Accountability.
Stay true to your faith and business principles, ensuring accountability to God, yourself, and your stakeholders. Transparent leadership builds trust and credibility.

8. Persevere with Purpose.
Challenges are inevitable, but faith and resilience turn obstacles into stepping stones. View difficulties as refining processes that strengthen your mission and leadership.

9. Invest in the Next Generation.
Mentorship and knowledge-sharing ensure that wisdom and values are passed on. Equip emerging entrepreneurs with

the skills and insights to lead businesses that prioritise impact over mere profit.

Reflections on the Angello Network and the Acts Community Values

Mason reflects on the Angello network's vision of 'doing business differently to bridge the gap between the rich and the poor.' He acknowledges the tension between *"what God wants us to do and what the world demands us to do,"* emphasising that Angello's approach is deeply rooted in stewardship, servant leadership and faith-driven impact.

"I always remember this: Jesus' teaching is always upside down from the rest of the world. As a result, there will be tension."

This understanding helps frame the challenges that inevitably come with faith-driven decisions, as they often run counter to profit-based market expectations and traditional investor mindsets. Embracing purpose-driven entrepreneurship demands a change of mindset from the traditional business objective of profit maximization, Mason advocates for profit-optimizing — strategically using capital to grow businesses sustainably while benefiting all stakeholders, including employees, vendors, and the broader community. He emphasises that businesses should measure success not only in financial terms but also in intentional impact outcomes that contribute to human flourishing.

"Human flourishing is, I think, an important part of God's heartbeat for people."

Human flourishing, Mason explains, reflects God's desire for people to thrive and live with dignity. Restoration focuses on restoring individuals to God's image, in heart, behaviour, and purpose. This "pursuit of holiness" shapes his approach to leadership, requiring that biblical principles be applied consistently in daily work to become Christ-like, continuing to carry out Jesus' declared mission to 'proclaim good news to the poor, freedom for the prisoner, recovery of sight for the blind, set the oppressed free, and proclaim the year of the Lord's favour.'

"I think the Jubilee gospel is as real as to me today, as when first preached by Jesus."

"It requires intentionality, applying what you learn in the Bible not just in theory, but in your actions at work — extending patience, showing grace, and seeking to serve others in all aspects of business."

Mason also highlights that aligning faith with business means intentionally creating systems that prioritize societal benefit. Capital is a resource for impact, rather than merely a profit-generating vehicle. His approach reflects a broader framework of stakeholder capitalism, where businesses are designed to serve communities, elevate human dignity, and empower vulnerable groups, while maintaining long-term financial sustainability.

This perspective informs how Mason leads the Garden Impact Fund and mentors others. He believes that entrepreneurship should be relational and redemptive, blending financial sustainability with ethical stewardship, purpose-driven impact, and community transformation. By integrating faith, intentionality and measurable impact into business, Mason demonstrates how living and working according to Christian principles not only guide decision-making, investment strategy, and the develop future leaders, it also contributes towards a satisfying, meaningful life for oneself.

"I strongly encourage Christian entrepreneurs, Christian businesspeople, believers, fellow believers and disciples to live out that faith with not just ... a superficial smile, but with really a deep joy and contentment."

"First of all, we are called to be content with what we have. And I think simplicity, be humble, you know, be modest and

be discreet, because Paul calls us to live a quiet yet impactful life."

Future Vision

During the COVID 19 pandemic Mason Tan wrote his first book, 'From Brokenness to Breakthrough', which tells the story of his spiritual transformation and his transition to the Kingdom work of social impact. He is about to publish a second book which explores how to follow the biblical commands and apply the Jubilee gospel to "*unlock*" the world from the shackles of its own greed. At the time of this interview, Mason was thinking of calling it 'The Spirituality of Investing in the Poor.' Although the wealth in the world has grown substantially in the past 10 to 15 years, the distribution of wealth is increasingly "*skewed towards the rich.*" The book explores how to be responsible stewards of this wealth by using biblical principles to "*show people what God really wants us to do with these financial resources*" and how they can use the talents they have been given to "*narrow the gap and make this world a better place to live in.*"

Looking ahead, Mason is passionate about mentoring and equipping the next generation of entrepreneurs to build businesses that prioritise people, purpose and impact. He believes that by sharing knowledge and resources, business leaders can create a ripple effect of positive transformation.

Mason hopes to continue demonstrating that it is possible to do good and do well at the same time, although it is unclear yet as to the future of the Garden Impact Fund.

"*It's actually meant to be a close-ended fund. We have gone through the first seven years cycle, and we have already had some partial exits of the earlier portfolio investments and the ones remaining are still doing well. We're still discussing about whether to expand more and become a perpetual fund or evergreen fund, or actually, maybe it's time to exit and do something else. It's a happy problem that we have. At this juncture, we want to see the Lord leading us into the next phase."*

Mason is committed to living out his faith through his work and supporting initiatives that create sustainable change.
"We need to reclaim the authenticity of the Gospel. The Gospel came down to save us. It is not just a theory, and we need to live out that faith."

Closing Reflections on the Conversation

In his closing reflections, Mason underscores the centrality of living out one's faith with authenticity, humility, and intentionality. He stresses that being a true follower of Jesus Christ extends beyond rituals, church attendance, or even visible acts of service; it is founded upon aligning one's heart, motives, and daily actions with God's calling.

"The question I ask myself: Am I a fake disciple? ... Am I a fake father? Am I a fake husband? The truth is, you may be appearing to do so many things that relate to the Kingdom of God, but what is your motivation? What is the heart of doing it?"

He encourages fellow entrepreneurs to examine the depth and authenticity of their faith, ensuring that their work is not merely performative but genuinely shaped by Christian values and spiritual growth. Mason is not afraid to reveal where he finds himself:

"... Only we know the answers, and God is interested to you know, help us to turn from being a goat to a sheep, and I think a sheep will hear God's voice and follow Him ... I'm not intimidated by the questions ... but one of the answers is, I have to shift my mindset from Jesus being my Saviour, to Jesus is my master. Jesus is my Saviour. I have to shift the mindset to Jesus is my master. I think I have come to a new season of my life. I need really to reflect, 'Am I really a follower of Jesus Christ, or am I just talk only?'"

Mason emphasises that leadership and impact are inseparable from service, sacrifice and accountability. True leadership, he argues, involves stewarding resources wisely, serving others selflessly, and making decisions guided by purpose rather than convenience.

"People ask me whether 'Am I a blessed Christian or a broken Christian?' And my answer is this: I'm a broken Christian because only God is good and the rest of us are imperfect, but because of his daily redeeming grace and mercies, I'm able to be blessed by Him every day, every hour and every minute, and therefore I Have hope. He is the path. Jesus is the path to the eternal home."

This acknowledgment of human imperfection is not resignation but a call to constant growth, humility, and dependence on God. He highlights the joy and contentment that come from aligning work with faith and purpose, even amidst the challenges. Success is measured not solely by financial returns but by human flourishing, redemption, and the positive transformation of communities. Mason's reflections serve as a reminder that the pursuit of holiness, integrity and impact in business requires courage, patience, and steadfastness.

Ultimately, Mason invites fellow entrepreneurs to integrate faith authentically into their professional lives: To walk the talk, to lead with integrity, and to embrace the calling to use business as a platform for redemptive, sustainable impact. He reminds leaders that it is through service, accountability and relational engagement that true restoration, both personal and societal, occurs.

Appendix One: Contributors

Profile

Malcolm Johnston & Artem Magay
Partner of Angello
Founder of Tribe

Malcolm Johnston lives in Ireland and is a Partner in Angello which was birthed in 2008. He was formerly CEO of a specialist investment management business with funds now of over £1bn. Malcolm has 40+ years of experience in frontier communities and markets, building NGOs and enterprise-led development projects. Angello Network is a fellowship of 20+ local, national level, visionary leaders in 12+ frontier nations. Malcolm is passionate that the vision of these leaders is heard and supported.

LinkedIn: www.linkedin.com/in/malcolm-johNston-3658461a

Company: Angello

Website: www.angello.com

Artem Magay Bio:

Company: Tribe

Websites:
https://www.instagram.com/artemm.inst/
https://www.instagram.com/tashkent_tribe/

Profile

Paul Lindsay & Roy Crowne
*Founder of Gospel Entrepreneurs,
Director of Angello Development Foundation.*

Paul Lindsay was educated in Belfast, Northern Ireland until 1981 and then spent a year volunteering with Operation Mobilisation in Khartoum, Sudan.

After completing a BSc in Quantity Surveying at Thames Polytechnic in London, Paul worked in the construction industry in London for over thirty-five years with several FTSE100 companies across numerous sectors.

He is a fellow of the Royal Institution of Chartered Surveyors, a trustee of Angello Development Foundation and the chair of the board for YFC Moscow Region, Russia. Paul is married to Mary and they have three adult children, Kathryn, Alex and Imogen.

LinkedIn: www.linkedin.com/in/paullindsay

Website: www.angello.com

Roy Crowne grew up in London's East End, trained as an engineer, and played rugby before a life-changing experience gave him lasting purpose.

Passionate about raising up the next generation of gospel-driven entrepreneurs, he co-founded Hope 08 and later served as Executive Director of HOPE until 2021, when he launched Gospel Entrepreneurs. This fast-growing initiative equips Christians to lead in church, ministry, and business with creativity and faith.

Previously, Roy spent 28 years with Youth for Christ—13 as National Director—and played a key role in uniting churches for mission through HOPE. Married to Flossie Crowne, has two grown-up children and two grandchildren.

LinkedIn: www.linkedin.com/in/roy-crowne-2253061b

Company: Gospel Entrepreneurs

Websites:
www.Gospelentrepreneurs.org
www.hopetogether.org.uk
www.revelationtrust.org

Profile

Ralph Catto, Luvuyo Rani & Colin Habberton
Principal of Guiding Capital
Co-Founder & CEO of Silulo Foundation
Co-founder & CEO of Relativ Impact

Ralph Catto is a Scottish entrepreneur and investor committed to blending social impact with commercial strategy. He began his career in corporate finance at a London stockbroking firm before founding a software start-up focused on social housing. Ralph is an active investor, focusing on businesses that drive meaningful social impact. He has served as a trustee of the Transformational Business Network, (TBN) a Christian-founded but non-discriminatory organization that empowers enterprises in developing countries to lift communities out of poverty. His work has taken him to Africa and the Balkans. In addition, he has been a trustee of local charities with a Matthew 15:31 focus and has played active roles in supporting church operations (behind the scenes).

LinkedIn: https://www.linkedin.com/in/ralph-catto-1824a7/

Company: Guiding Capital

Website: https://www.guidingcapital.co.uk

Luvuyo Rani was born in Queenstown and is now based in the Western Cape, Luvuyo is a visionary leader and award-winning entrepreneur with a B.Tech from the University of Cape Town's Graduate School of Business. Luvuyo is the Founder and CEO of Silulo Ulutho Technologies, a pioneering social enterprise bridging the digital divide across South Africa. His dedication to inclusive digital access has earned him global recognition, including being named one of the JCI Ten Outstanding Young Persons of the World (2014) and a Schwab Foundation Social Entrepreneur (2016).

LinkedIn: https://www.linkedin.com/in/luvuyo-rani-0415701b/

Company: Silulo Foundation

Website: https://silulofoundation.org/

Colin Habberton is a Co-Founder and Executive Director of the Relativ Group, an impact solutions provider based in Cape Town, South Africa, with subsidiaries in Canada, United Kingdom and New Zealand. Relativ Impact serves investors, corporates, social enterprises, foundations, government agencies and nonprofits in over 50 countries.

Colin and his multi-disciplinary global team have spent more than 15 years developing tools, processes and plans that guide organisations to identify, manage and amplify their impact. He is a Fellow of the Institute of Directors South Africa, a Fellow of the Royal Society for the Encouragement of Arts, Manufactures and Commerce (UK), and an Endeavor mentor.

Colin holds a PhD in Business Management & Administration. His PhD research focused on the decision-making dynamics of institutional investors towards responsible investing. He has contributed to a variety of industry and media reviews and presented at global conferences on impact management, finance, analytics, decision-making, fundraising, strategic communications and systems change.

LinkedIn: https://www.linkedin.com/in/colin-habberton-22b0411/

Company: Relativ Impact

Website: www.relativimpact.com

Profile

Reuben Coulter
Founder of Ignis Global

Reuben Coulter is founder of Ignis Global, an impact investment advisory which serves family offices and foundations. He is a Senior Advisor to Faith Driven Investor, a Senior Fellow at Belmont University and an Associate of Angello Network.
Prior to this, he was CEO of Transformational Business Network, a global impact investment network, and a Fellow and Associate Director for Africa at the World Economic Forum in Switzerland. He was also the founding CEO of Tearfund Ireland, part of Tearfund UK's Disaster Management Team in Liberia, DRC and Darfur, and Chair of the Irish Humanitarian Committee.

Reuben completed an Executive Masters in Leadership with Wharton, Colombia, London and INSEAD Business Schools and a Masters in Public Health at the London School of Hygiene and Tropical Medicine.

LinkedIn: http://www.linkedin.com/in/reubencoulter

Company: Ignis

Websites:
Faith Driven Investor http://www.faithdriveninvestor.org
Angello Network http://www.angello.com/
Weller's Impact Investment http://www.wellersimpact.com/
FORGE Global Summit Forge Global Summit 2025
https://www.forgemovement.org/

Profile
Duncan Parker & Kehkshan Newton
CEO of The 44 Group
Head of Business Development of Pak Mission Society

Duncan Parker brings a unique blend of experience across the third sector and private sector, leveraging commercial solutions to address critical social and environmental challenges. Passionate about driving a triple bottom line—People, Planet, and Profit—he is committed to fostering sustainable and scalable impact that promotes human flourishing.

His career began in humanitarian aid and development, where he led the development arm of one of the world's most recognised international NGOs. Transitioning into the emerging field of impact investing, Duncan played a pivotal role in connecting purpose-driven businesses with much-needed capital. As the leader of a private equity-backed firm, he helped raise over £150 million for mission-driven enterprises and charities.

Following the sale of the business in 2023, Duncan now leads The 44 Group, a private family office dedicated to investing in businesses that create meaningful, lasting change for human flourishing.

LinkedIn: https://www.linkedin.com/in/duncan-parker-366bb68/

Company: The 44 Group

Website: https://www.the44group.co.uk/

Kehkshan Newton has been working with Pak Mission Society and has led the Entrepreneurial Journey through a remarkable transformation from a traditional humanitarian aid organization to a dynamic, hybrid enterprise model. Under her leadership, the organization has built a thriving entrepreneurial ecosystem that now supports over 10,000 entrepreneurs across Pakistan.

LinkedIn: https://www.linkedin.com/in/kehkshan-newton-952a40136/

Company: Pak Mission Society

Website: www.pakmissionsociety.org

Profile

Hakan Sandberg & Manpan Wungak
Founder of Itzinya Networks
Co-Founder Itzinya Nigeria

Hakan Sandberg is a Swedish entrepreneur and founder of the Itzinya network, Prior to launching Itzinya, Hakan was the founder and CEO of a top-ranked soft skills company in Turkey, serving Fortune 100 and Fortune 500 companies with leadership development and personal and team effectiveness training. With over 20 years of experience in leadership and personal development, he is also a certified business coach and has successfully founded multiple businesses in Sweden and internationally.

LinkedIn: www.linkedin.com/in/håkan-hakan sandberg-31820810

Dr. Manpan Joseph Wungak was born 5th Feb. 1969. Nigerian, is a Veterinary Surgeon with over 20years 'practice experience, a Project Manager and an entrepreneur passionate about sustainable business development. His passion is mentoring and coaching young entrepreneurs with Big Dreams and innovative value propositions. He is a Consultant on innovation and Design Thinking. His Vision is an empowered continent through generational chains of successful entrepreneurs with huge resources all over Africa

LinkedIn: www.linkedin.com/in/manpan4wungak

Company: Itzinya Networks

Website: www.itzinya.org

Profile

Nikolaus Hutter & Edson Niwamanya
Partner & Founder of New Paradigm Ventures
Investment and Operations Lead, Uganda

Nikolaus Hutter is the founder of New Paradigm Ventures, an international advisory firm, focused on accelerating the shift to a purpose-driven economy, by prototyping it today.

He advises international NGOs on Impact Ventures & Investment, and works with impact entrepreneurs around the globe to develop and scale business and investment models to address issues in the blind spots of our economy: the people, places and topics that markets neglect.

He initiated the first accelerator for social innovators in Central Europe and led the impact investor network Toniic in Europe, and serves on the Board of impact funds in Europe and East Africa, and impact investor networks in Greece and Hungary. Prior to founding NPV in 2010, he worked in the VC industry for over a decade, and as a strategy consultant. He read economics in Vienna, Strasburg and at LSE.

LinkedIn: www.linkedin.com/in/nikolaushutter

Edson Niwamanya is an impact-driven leader in social entrepreneurship and impact finance. His mission is to unlock the right type of capital for underserved entrepreneurs, enabling them to grow and scale solutions that address urgent social and environmental challenges. He is committed to reimagining how early-stage businesses are funded by advancing models that balance purpose with profitability.
Over the course of his career, Edson has supported social ventures in refining their business models, securing investment, and expanding their impact. As Co-founder and Investment Lead at Relevant Ventures, he develops and manages innovative approaches to impact financing.

Beyond his venture work, Edson actively contributes to the entrepreneurial ecosystem as a mentor, trainer, and speaker with both local and international programs.

LinkedIn: https://www.linkedin.com/in/niwamanya-edson-7a32bb13b/

Company: Relevant

Website: https://www.relevant.is/

Profile

Derek Kessen & Anatol Malancea
Managing Partner of Heron Group
Co-founder and CEO of Uniqa Wall Systems

Derek Kessen is the Managing Partner of Heron Group, a management consulting and investment management firm based in Chicago with offices in Nairobi, Kenya. With clients and investments in over 40 countries across Africa, Asia, and the Americas, Derek is passionate about the role of business in delivering economic and social outcomes within both developed and developing communities.

Before founding Heron Group in 2020, Derek spent 13 years at Performance Trust Capital Partners in Chicago, where he specialised in building investment portfolio strategies for banks and credit unions. With a total of 19 years of experience in the global capital markets, his expertise includes portfolio management, change management and strategic decision-making. Derek earned a degree in Finance from the University of Missouri and later an MBA from Kellogg School of Management at Northwestern University. His career has been defined by a commitment to impactful investment strategies and a focus on fostering growth that benefits people and businesses across the globe.

LinkedIn: www.linkedin.com/in/derekkessen

Company: Heron Group is a management consulting and investment management firm that expands the transformational influence of redemptive companies through growth and investment strategies. Founded in 2020, the company's advisory group works shoulder-to-shoulder with middle market businesses on their most expensive problems. With clients ranging from $100M to 10B in revenue, Heron Consulting helps companies address areas of strategic growth, operational effectiveness, and organizational health. In 2021, the team launched Heron Ventures, an investment manager that builds professional pathways of investing in early and growth stage businesses in overlooked communities. As a professional capital allocator, Heron Ventures manages three private investment funds with a geographic footprint in East Africa, Eastern Europe, and Central Asia. The company has offices in Chicago, USA and Nairobi, Kenya.

Website: www.herongroup.co

Anatol Malancea is a visionary entrepreneur and impact-driven business leader, serving as the Co-founder and CEO of Uniqa Wall Systems, an innovative modular housing company in Moldova producing energy-efficient, factory-made homes for the European market.

With over a decade of experience in international sales and corporate leadership at prestigious companies such as Swarovski and Schonbek Worldwide Lighting, Anatol brings a wealth of expertise in business development, market expansion and forging strategic partnerships.

A graduate of the Academy of Economic Studies of Moldova in Business and Economics, he has further strengthened his expertise through executive training in the US, Canada, and Switzerland. Anatol has built a global network of partners through leadership roles, business ventures, and social impact initiatives. Beyond business, he chairs Communitas NGO, supporting young entrepreneurs, vulnerable children and communities in Moldova and most recently playing an active role in the Ukrainian refugee crisis.

A frequent traveller between Europe and the U.S., Anatol is passionate about transformational investing, ecosystem building, and fostering sustainable economic development in Moldova and beyond. His leadership and dedication position him as a key player in both business and social impact circles.

LinkedIn: www.linkedin.com/in/malancea-anatol-31a3061

Company: Uniqa Wall Systems is a modular housing company specializing in energy-efficient, in factory-made, lego-type homes for the European market. Based in Moldova, Uniqa delivers sustainable, high-performance, and seismically resilient homes to markets in the Netherlands, Germany, Romania, and Ukraine.

With a focus on innovation and eco-friendly construction, Uniqa reduces CO_2 emissions while ensuring rapid, high-quality assembly. Beyond housing, the company drives local job creation and economic growth, making sustainable living more accessible.

Website: www.uniqa.md

Profile
Ruben Marian & Daniel Lar
Co-founders of GUILD

Ruben Marian is a Christ-centred entrepreneur from Cluj-Napoca, Romania, passionate about driving transformation through business and leadership. With a background in Computer Science, he and his wife, Oana, co-founded UTILBEN, a leading provider of heavy machinery, and have since expanded their investments into agriculture, dermato-cosmetics, and tourism, while also mentoring and investing in young entrepreneurs.

Ruben co-founded GUILD, a movement which equips leaders for urban mission and discipleship, and actively supports Angello Network and Forge Movement, fostering entrepreneurial ecosystems in emerging and frontier nations.

Through his work, Ruben empowers leaders to integrate Kingdom principles into business, influence culture, and create lasting impact in society. Outside of business and leadership, he enjoys traveling and outdoor adventures with Oana, celebrating and contributing to God's redemptive work in the world.

LinkedIn: www.linkedin.com/in/rubenmarian

Daniel Lar is a seasoned portfolio manager at Total Specific Solutions, a division of Constellation Software. He is also the co-founder of Guild and the initiator of the Timothy Urban Mission Training Program, dedicated to equipping individuals for impactful community service. In addition to his work in the business sector, Daniel is an investor in SaladBox, supporting innovation in the food industry.

Beyond his professional pursuits, he serves as a pastor at Teofania Church, where he is committed to spiritual leadership and community development.

LinkedIn: www.linkedin.com/in/daniellar

Company: GUILD is a movement of Christian leaders committed to integrating faith, values, and purpose into every aspect of life. Our mission is to equip and empower leaders to be ambassadors of Christ, making disciples and transforming society through Kingdom values.

Websites:
www.guild.ro
www.utilben.ro
www.regivero.ro
https://www.facebook.com/TeofaniaRo/

Additional associations: Timothy Program is a transformational journey for Christians seeking clarity on their identity, mission, and calling in God's Kingdom. It equips leaders to integrate faith with career, actively build the Body of Christ, and influence society through discipleship, leadership, and mission.

Website: https://2tim22.co

Profile
Smily Rostus
Managing Director

Dr. Smily Rostus is a visionary leader committed to enabling mission-driven organizations to achieve transformative impact. By reimagining systems, unlocking potential, and nurturing entrepreneurial drive, he seeks to spark a wave of renewal that resonates from local communities to global movements.

As the Managing Director of SUREnterprise in New Delhi, India, Dr. Rostus guides a diverse group of companies in microfinance, veterinary services, technology, and AgTech, driving them toward sustainable growth and meaningful impact.

Previously, he served as CEO of HillTree Consulting Group, where he spearheaded enterprise strategy, transformation, ESG initiatives, and consulting services. His career began in the banking and insurance sectors, with roles at globally renowned institutions such as HSBC, AIG, and MetLife in India and the Middle East.

Beyond his corporate roles, Dr. Rostus is passionately engaged in the nonprofit sector, serving as the National Treasurer of INTERSERVE India, where he advances its mission-focused goals. He also serves as a trustee for the Centre for Housing and Community Development, focusing on affordable housing and skill development.

Additionally, he contributes to the leadership teams of Angello Network and FORGE movement, supporting faith-driven entrepreneurial ecosystems in emerging and frontier nations.

Smily is also a member of the Christian Economic Forum (CEF) that believes in the vision of solving the world's greatest problems through God inspired solutions.

Outside of his professional endeavours, Dr. Rostus cherishes moments spent with his family, including his wife, Shiney Rostus, and their daughters, Sharon (13) and Shannon (11), finding fulfillment in their shared experiences.

LinkedIn: www.linkedin.com/in/smilyrostus

Company: Shikhar Urban and Rural Enterprises Private Limited (SUREnterprise)
Website: www.surenterprise.com

Company: Hill Tree Global
Website: www.hilltreeglobal.com

Profile

David Harlley & Keren Pybus
Co-Founder & CEO of ThirdWay Capital
Co-Founder & CEO of Ethical Apparel

David Harlley is an accomplished business leader, engineer, and start-up coach with a diverse background spanning engineering, corporate strategy, and impact investment. He began his career as a design engineer and project manager in the construction industry, managing medium and large-scale mechanical-electrical projects across sectors such as healthcare, transit, commercial and residential.

Before co-founding Third Way Capital, David held executive roles at engineering firm WSP, where he specialized in corporate restructuring and strategy while leading regional operations. His expertise in navigating complex business environments and driving organizational growth has been a defining feature of his career.

David holds an MBA from the prestigious IE Business School in Madrid, Spain, and has achieved both levels of the Chartered Alternative Investment Analyst (CAIA) designation. In addition to his professional roles, he serves as an adjunct lecturer at IE University, where he teaches on the topic of Distributive Capitalism, reflecting his commitment to innovative economic models that drive equitable and sustainable impact. His newly released book, "Building The New Economy - Distributive Capitalism", outlines the potential of diverse and decentralized ownership to remedy areas of economic dysfunction, including wealth inequality, and environmental degradation.

LinkedIn: www.linkedin.com/in/davidharlley

Company: ThirdWay Capital

Website: www.thirdwaycapital.co

Keren Pybus is the Co-founder and CEO of Ethical Apparel Africa (EAA), bringing over 25 years of experience in sourcing, merchandising, and retail operations. Driven by a passion for ethical manufacturing, she co-founded EAA with Paloma to demonstrate that living wages and worker empowerment can go hand in hand with cost-competitive production and profitability.

Keren has worked across the globe, including three years in Bangladesh where she established and managed the George Clothing sourcing office. Her experience spans collaborations with major retailers such as Walmart UK and South Africa, as well as partnerships with small-scale artisan suppliers. Now based in London, she travels frequently to Ghana where EAA's main operations are located.

EAA is an apparel sourcing and manufacturing company with an innovative operating model that prioritizes both product quality and worker well-being. With a decade of experience exporting to the US, EU, and UK, EAA is set to export $8 million this year. The company operates primarily in Ghana where it is the majority-owner of Maagrace, a factory employing 750 people, and partners closely with three additional factories. Through ethical practices and strategic partnerships, Keren continues to drive meaningful change in the global apparel industry.

LinkedIn: www.linkedin.com/in/keren-pybus-68b4188

Company: Ethical Apparel

Website: www.ethicalapparelafrica.com

# Profile
Mason Tan
Director: Impact Investing

Mason Tan is a pioneer in social impact investing with over 35 years of international experience in finance and entrepreneurship. As the Director of Impact Investing at Providentia Wealth Advisory, a regulated fund manager in Singapore, he oversees the Garden Impact Fund, which is an impact-driven investment vehicle supporting scalable businesses that drive social change across Southeast Asia.

A graduate of the University of Southern California with a B.Sc. and a Masters in Accounting, Mason has worked across the U.S., Indonesia, Singapore, and China. In 2013, he co-founded Garden Impact Investments Pte Ltd and Transformational Business Network Asia (TBN Asia), both of which focus on addressing poverty through sustainable business solutions.

Mason also serves on the global board of directors of Prison Fellowship International (PFI), leveraging his expertise in finance, accounting and impact investing to drive innovative approaches to blended economic development and social transformation.

The Garden Impact Fund (GIF), Singapore's first social impact Variable Capital Company (VCC), is managed by Providentia Wealth Advisory Ltd. It seeks to improve the quality of life for vulnerable communities in Southeast Asia by creating sustainable economic opportunities and increasing access to essential services. GIF invests in scalable businesses that generate measurable social impact, particularly in the circular economy, healthcare, training, and employment sectors. Beyond financial investment, GIF takes a long-term, hands-on approach, providing strategic guidance, expertise, and access to its extensive global and regional networks.

LinkedIn: www.linkedin.com/in/mason-tan-0449397

Company: Garden Impact Fund
Website: www.gardenimpactfund.com

Company: Providentia Wealth Advisory Ltd
Website: www.providentiawealth.com

Company: Transformational Business Network Asia (TBN Asia)
Website: www.tbn.asia

Printed in Dunstable, United Kingdom